GHOSTBELLY

GHOSTBELLY

Elizabeth Heineman

THE
FEMINIST PRESS
AT THE CITY UNIVERSITY
OF NEW YORK
NEW YORK CITY

Published in 2014 by the Feminist Press
at the City University of New York
The Graduate Center
365 Fifth Avenue, Suite 5406
New York, NY 10016

feministpress.org

First printing March 2014

Cover design by Herb Thornby
Text design by Drew Stevens

Library of Congress Cataloging-in-Publication Data

Heineman, Elizabeth D., 1962-
Ghostbelly / Elizabeth Heineman.
    pages cm
Includes bibliographical references and index.
ISBN 978-1-55861-844-2 (alk. paper)
1. Heineman, Elizabeth D., 1962- 2. Stillbirth. 3. Infants—Death.
4. Loss (Psychology) 5. Bereavement. I. Title.
RG631.H45 2014
618.3'92—dc23
                                            2013035187

For Thor.
It's no substitute for a life.

I believe that people should have control of what information about them is made public. For this reason, I have changed many names in this book, leaving original names only for those who explicitly expressed their comfort with that arrangement.

I

Sites of Memory

IT WAS ALL SO LONG AGO. IT WAS JUST YESTERDAY. I watch Glenn, the midwife, myself as if through a thick window, out of reach. The screams and moans muffled, the light distorted by the mottled, wavy glass against which I press my face. I pound my fists on the window, shout at them, try to warn them, but they do not hear. My hips are compact inside my shorts, my trunk limber as it leans forward to write. My belly does not remember; only some deep and tight part of my throat does.

I SIT on the living room sofa, under the dark window. Glenn and I have finished dinner, and we're both looking at our laptops. Glenn is checking email, and I'm catching up with post-election episodes of *The Daily Show*. It is November 11, 2008. I'm in labor, but I don't tell Glenn.

We are alone. Adam, sixteen, had been with us for a week and a half, but Julia, his other mother, came back from her travels last night, and now Adam is at her house. We're enjoying the quiet, and from the time Adam left for school that morning, we've shared a sense of relaxed excitement, knowing we are in the final stages of waiting.

My contractions are mild, little bits of tightening, very short, not at all painful. But they are regular. I have a piece of paper next to me, on the arm of the sofa, and on it I write down the times of my contractions. I'll do this for a while and then let Glenn in on the secret. My feet are propped up on a footstool. Glenn's feet are stretched across the sofa toward me. Every now and then I rub his feet a little. Then I take my right hand back to note the time of the latest contraction.

I tell Glenn after an hour or so. His face jolts into a smile. I tell him these are just little contractions, but they're regular; this is definitely labor. He asks if we should call Deirdre, our midwife. Not yet, I say. I haven't been paying attention to how long the contractions are, and she'll want to know that. Let me time a few of them and then we'll call her.

I'M IN the kitchen, pacing. I have put water on for tea and a slice of bread in the toaster. I'll need to have energy for the birth; I should eat now while I can. I've phoned Julia to let her know I'm in labor. As I pace, I read a book. During my early labor with Adam, I'd played Tetris on the computer, until the contractions kept ruining my score.

Glenn is running up and down the stairs. He's setting up the aqua doula.

I eat my toast, I drink my tea, I read my book, I time my contractions. After half an hour, I know how long they are. Twenty-five to thirty seconds. I call Deirdre. It's shortly after 10:37. That's the time of the last contraction I write down.

I AM on the phone with Deirdre. She tells me she is not at home: she's finishing up at Katie and Joe's place. They just had a baby girl. I tell her we'd had a bet on whose baby would come first—Katie and Joe had been in our birthing class. "Well, you lost that one," Deirdre laughs. She tells me she'll be over in twenty minutes.

DEIRDRE KNEELS at the end of my bed. I am on my back, and she's examining me. "Baby's got a good heartbeat," she says. "Let's look inside."

Deirdre puts on a glove and feels around. "Two centimeters dilated, 80 percent effaced," she says. "Just like at your checkup yesterday." She withdraws her hand. "But take a look at this!" She shows me her gloved hand, smeared with dark blood. "That's your bloody show," she says. "Things are definitely happening." She snaps off the glove. "It's going to be a while—you're only at two centimeters. No birthday today. But tomorrow, definitely."

Glenn asks if it's too early to set up the aqua doula.

"No," Deirdre says, "go ahead and fill it. The heating element will keep it warm, so it'll be ready whenever we are."

Deirdre tells me she's going to go home to get some rest for my delivery. I should call her when the contractions are sixty seconds long, or if my water breaks. She lives two blocks away. Once I call, she'll be over in five minutes.

I LIE in bed, on my side. I am angry at Glenn, and he is angry at me, though we are both trying not to be angry. I'm angry because he is typing emails. He needs to let people at work know that I'm in labor and he won't be in for the next couple of days. He types many emails: to his graduate class, the departmental secretary, his chair, his teaching assistant. I've asked if he can't just let the secretary know, and tell her who else needs to be informed. That's why he's angry with me. I always have ideas about how he can do things more efficiently.

My contractions are getting stronger. Really, they stopped being mild not long after Deirdre left. I'm curled on my side, my back to Glenn, who is perched on the side of the bed. When I have a contraction, I groan and writhe, and Glenn reaches his arm backward to stroke me. When a contraction is over, he gives my arm a squeeze and goes back to typing.

I am trying to nap between contractions. If you begin labor as night falls, you want to get some sleep, so you haven't missed a whole night when things get intense. But my contractions are close together, and I'm doubtful it will work. Still, a couple of times a contraction jolts me into consciousness, and so I know I must have dozed off.

Glenn snaps his laptop shut. Should he take it downstairs, he asks, or just set it aside up here to stay with me? I tell him to take it downstairs. I don't want him to be tempted to check his email later on if things take a while.

Later, I will become convinced that is was during this time, while I lay on my side and contractions grew strong faster than I expected, that Thor began to die inside me. It will gnaw at me that Glenn was typing emails while Thor was dying, though there's not a thing he could have done about it.

I FEEL the tile floor under my feet in the bathroom. I've moved there because I wanted to squeeze a trip to the toilet in between contractions, but I don't go back to bed. A little blood trickled down the inside of my leg when I got up. After I pee, another contraction comes, and with it more blood. I clean it up with toilet paper and think: if there's blood, I should stay here, that will make it easier to clean up after each contraction. And it seems better to stand during these contractions, since standing allows me to move. The light in the bathroom is too bright and it reflects glaringly against the hard, white floor tiles. The window next to the toilet shows a rectangle of perfect darkness. It's a clinical space: gleaming white tiles, bright red spots of blood on the tiles, sharp light.

Glenn comes to support me during a contraction, kisses my face, helps to clean up the blood. The contractions had gotten stronger while I lay in bed, but now that I am standing, they cut like a knife. I scream. Once, I moan, "God, this hurts so much." But I know it'll be over soon. Each contraction will be over in a few seconds. And the whole thing won't last more than a few hours. I'd screamed during Adam's birth, too. It had helped to let the pain go through me and out with the air, rather than trying to contain it.

Glenn asks whether we should be concerned about the blood. I tell him that birth involves blood, and he believes me, because I've had a baby before. He times my contractions: forty seconds, forty-five—nowhere near sixty. He tries to apply pressure to my lower back during a contraction. One of the birthing books had said the partner should do that. We'd both hated that book—it made the woman a helpless creature who needed to be managed by her husband (always a husband)—but perhaps the low-back pressure is a good idea. It isn't. It makes the pain worse. I tell him to stop.

I lean on the bathroom counter under the fluorescent lights, pace, hang on to Glenn's neck. More blood, more toilet paper to wipe it up and flush it away. After a couple more contractions I tell him I don't like this bleeding, it's too much. He should call Deirdre.

I AM on my back, in bed. Deirdre is checking things out. She is alarmed by the blood. She is not alarmed that she can't find a heartbeat in the few seconds before my next contraction comes. It can be hard to find a heartbeat as the baby is descending and changing its position, never mind if the mother is squirming about. But she is very alarmed by what she finds inside. I am dilated to eight centimeters. I was two centimeters barely two hours ago. My body is trying to get the baby out fast, because the baby is in trouble.

Deirdre tells me she's going to break my water. I am disappointed. Adam was born with his amniotic sac intact. It had burst as he'd come out. The Berlin midwife had told us that was traditionally seen as a sign of good luck. The baby is well protected even coming out of the womb. It will be loved and cherished all its life. I'd liked that.

I have a contraction. Deirdre tells me she'll reach a long hook in, like a crochet hook, and snag the sac to break it. I don't see what comes out, but Glenn does, and later he tells me: it was muddy, dark brown, with chunks, like diarrhea.

Deirdre tells me we needed to get this baby out *now*. I am to push with all my might. No more screaming, the energy has to go into pushing. Glenn is to go to her car and bring up the oxygen tank—she'd left it there in her rush to get to me right away. She might need to do a resuscitation. Once he gets back, she says, he should get the phone and be ready to call 911.

A contraction comes. I push. Pushing without screaming

feels purposeful. I'm not letting the pain run through me; I'm using it. But the contraction ends, and the baby is not out. "Push, Lisa," Deirdre says, "get this baby out." Another contraction, another push, no baby. "I'm going to make a cut, Lisa, to help the baby come out faster." I'd had a cut with Adam, I don't mind. Deirdre reaches for her scissors. But first: another contraction, another push, baby. Slithering out, like a bumpy, slimy fish. Deirdre tells Glenn, who has just run up the stairs with the oxygen, to call 911.

DEIRDRE PICKS up Thor, practically tosses him onto my chest. I am still. My job is to be still and let Deirdre do her work. I hold Thor with my right arm but look at the ceiling. Deirdre listens for a heartbeat and finds none. She tries to resuscitate him. She suctions his nose, presses his chest, breathes into his nose and mouth. She does this over and over. I lay still, feeling the absence of pain, knowing that to be able to lie still because there is no more pain is important.

Later I will realize that I missed my one chance to look closely at Thor, to really take him in, in his natural state, without intubation tubes or pegs in his legs, without stitches from the autopsy, without skin made hard because his blood had been replaced by embalming fluid. Instead, I look at the ceiling.

I HEAR Glenn calling 911. He has been confused, helpless. He'd thought labor would last a long time so he could write all his emails, but things had moved fast. He'd been concerned about the blood, but I'd told him it was OK. When Deirdre discovered I was at eight centimeters, he'd asked if he should check the aqua doula. "This isn't going to be a water birth," I'd told him. He'd seen the hideous meconium, heard the urgency in Deirdre's voice as she told me we were to get the baby out *now*, and asked if this would be a good time to get the camera. "No," Deirdre had said evenly but tensely, "this is not the time for a camera." He'd sat next to me on the bed, urging me to get into another position. If he knew anything from the birthing classes, it was that lying flat on your back is the worst way to have a baby. It's more painful if you can't move around, and you won't have gravity to help. With Adam, I'd perched on the edge of the bed, and Julia had supported me from behind. Perhaps I should do that now, with him. "Glenn," I'd said, "I'm not moving. I can't."

Now the baby is here and he's calling 911. "Tell them childbirth, full infant resuscitation," Deirdre says. Glenn tells them our address, he spells his name, he tells them our midwife is with us, he tells them our phone number, he tells them I'm not hemorrhaging, he tells them the baby was just born a moment ago. He tells them he can hear the sirens approaching. He hangs up. The flashing lights insinuate their way into the bedroom through the sole window.

I DO not see Thor on the kitchen counter, where the EMT people have taken him. Glenn sees, and he later tells me: Thor is splayed out on the white counter, as if he were on an operating table. It is a kitchen island, and the responders surround him from all sides. The bright ceiling lights, halogen bulbs, shine directly onto Thor and make it look even more like a hospital room. They have some equipment Deirdre does not have for pulling the fluid out of his lungs, and fluid gushes out. "So much fluid, so much," Glenn later says.

I am still in bed, upstairs. EMT personnel surround me, too, but there is nothing for them to do. I am not hemorrhaging. I have already delivered the placenta, painlessly, just a moment after I had delivered Thor, as I had with Adam. The placenta is in a steel bowl on the bathroom counter. Deirdre had told Glenn to get a bowl for it since the EMT people would want to take it to the hospital. Deirdre and the EMT people stand around.

Jeannie, the doula, is also there, also standing around. Jeannie lives much farther away than Deirdre does, and she arrived just as the ambulances were pulling up. Jeannie is six months pregnant with twins, but from where I lie, I cannot see her belly.

The stretcher bounces beneath me. I am being taken to the ambulance. The EMT people carry me down our narrow staircase, with a tight ninety-degree turn on the stretcher, and I am impressed. I recall the paramedics in Berlin carrying me up the steps of our fifth-floor walk-up in a transport chair after Adam was born, and having been even more impressed.

SNOW FALLS gently on my face as they take me to the ambulance. I lie still, as I had on the bed when Deirdre had tried to resuscitate Thor. My job remains to lie still and let others do their work. My body is exhausted and my mind numb, and so it is easy to lie still. The air is cold and the sky is dark. How strange, that light and dark, cold and hot, still exist. "Outdoors is different from indoors, just like it always is," I think idly, and feel the icy flecks of snow melt on my cheeks.

Glenn rides in the ambulance with me. He'd had a choice: in one ambulance with me, or in the other ambulance with

Thor. He'd chosen my ambulance, then nearly been left behind as he'd raced to make sure the cats were inside before locking the door. He was still confused; keeping the cats inside seemed very important. He'd hoped to sit with me, but that was not permitted. He had to sit in the front seat while a paramedic sat with me.

Glenn looks over his shoulder at me, and I look at him. Then I close my eyes, or look at the ceiling, or both, one after another, and say to myself, "OK, hospital people, now is your moment, do your magic, bring Thor back." I know that if Thor had been resuscitated, someone would have told me. He has been without a heartbeat much too long. But still, I tell the hospital people to do their magic.

A SWARM of medical personnel buzzes around my hospital bed. I can't tell one from another; they all wear light blue. My legs are in stirrups and I am shivering. I am wearing only a sweaty, brown tank top.

The swarm looks between my legs. One palpates my belly hard, pushes the residual blood out. It's clear that I am fine. I am not hemorrhaging. My blood pressure is normal. I can converse with them. I am freezing, but that is just because I have no blankets. They do not notice my shivering, because it is my upper body that is shivering, and they are looking at my lower body.

The swarm is stitching me up. My cervix tore a bit when I pushed Thor out at only eight centimeters.

The swarm asks: Do I want morphine?

"No," I say. They ask two more times, and I say no two more times. I will want to have my wits about me when the official word comes about Thor. Glenn and I will need to experience this together. I do not want to be drugged. I do not want to fade in and out, in one world, while Glenn is in another. Anyway, if you've just gone through natural childbirth, having your cervix stitched really doesn't hurt very much.

GLENN IS gone. He came up with me to this room, but he is no longer here. Not long after they started working on me, someone entered the room and said that they needed a parent to come with them to the emergency room to talk to the social worker and make some decisions. "A parent," as if Glenn and I might discuss it and decide which of us wanted to go. "Make decisions," as if there were any decisions to be made.

I know what "social worker" means. It means death.

Glenn will later tell me: the walk to the emergency room was surreal. The social worker asked how he was and talked about the weather and wondered where he worked. She was very young. Glenn didn't know what "social worker" meant, but he knew Thor was dead anyway.

The ER doctor meets Glenn outside the room where they'd worked on Thor. He starts explaining that when Thor had come in he had been without oxygen for a long time, that they had tried to somethingsomethingsomething.

Glenn interrupts him. "He didn't make it."

"No, he didn't," the doctor says. "You can go in and see him."

Thor is swaddled on the table, only his face showing. Glenn does not touch him. Glenn sits a moment, but feels uneasy. He shouldn't be here with Thor when I can't be there too. Someone, absurdly, brings him a glass of orange juice. Glenn asks to see the doctor. He asks the doctor if I will be able to see Thor as well. The doctor tells him I will. Glenn tells the doctor he is ready to leave the ER and go back to me.

GLENN SITS on the sofa in my hospital room. The sofa is under a window whose venetian blinds are drawn tightly, as if the bright light from outside might be disturbing. It is three a.m.

Glenn averts his face, turns it a little to the left and downward, closes his eyes. It's a gesture he makes in moments of extreme pain. I've only seen him do it one other time, when he was raw from contemplating his sister's diagnosis of early-onset Parkinson's.

"He didn't make it," Glenn says.

I hear myself say, "I'm sorry, I'm sorry, I'm sorry, I'm sorry."

I think it is my fault. I had wanted a home birth.

Glenn has always wanted children. He would be a wonderful father. He puts his family above all else. He dotes on his mother and his sister. He is calm and accepting of people's foibles. He doesn't expect people to be like him, or to be complementary to him, or to be anything other than what they are. He is gentle and completely generous. How many men who don't really want children, or who want them as long as they do most things right and don't get in the way too much, or who truly want and love the good and the bad but it turns out are willing to give up the day-to-day work if that's how things settle after the divorce—how many men like that have kids? Glenn has no kids.

I have Adam.

Glenn had a wife once. She didn't want children. Glenn had a pregnant girlfriend once. She didn't want children, at least not with him. Glenn always put his lovers first and worked to maintain the relationship without children, if that was how the women wanted it. You don't have kids as part of a couple unless both partners want them. As Glenn grew older, he didn't look for a woman ten or fifteen years younger so she could have children, so she could provide him with children. He didn't think that a relationship with that kind of age difference could be a relationship of equals.

Glenn joked that he'd spent years in therapy coming to terms with the fact that he was never going to have children.

Then I came along, and I wanted children, even though I had one who was practically grown. And I got pregnant, and the baby didn't have Down syndrome, and everything went beautifully. The baby grew and was strong, and I was healthy and fit, and we travelled, pregnant, to the East Coast and South Dakota and Wyoming and Vienna and Budapest and Lucerne and Copenhagen and Minneapolis. And I was so happy, so healthy and fit, that I wanted it to be just like last time with Adam, not in a hospital with the swarm between my legs, their eyes glued to a machine, looking for the sign that it was time to inject or test or cut, but just my lover and my midwife, strong enough to let me bear my pain, and our baby slipping into our arms.

Later I will understand that we couldn't automatically blame the home birth, that the matter was more complicated than that. But that is later.

I feel my lips and tongue moving, my throat vibrating. I

feel my eyelids pressing against my eyes. I feel nothing below my waist, because that part of my body is tired.

"I'm sorry, I'm sorry, I'm sorry, I'm sorry."

THE MAN from the medical examiner's office stands by my bed. He has come to tell me that there will be an autopsy because the death occurred outside the hospital. He has come to tell me that they can bring us the baby for a little while before they do the autopsy.

"How long?" I ask.

"About half an hour," he says.

It is four in the morning. I want Adam and Julia to see the baby. Julia will call at 6:30, when she wakes up, to find out how everything went. I will tell her then that Thor has died, and that she and Adam should come to the hospital to see him.

I tell this to the man from the medical examiner's office. I tell him I would like to have the baby longer, so my son can see him.

He tells me that is not possible. If I want anyone else to see the baby, I should call them now.

I cannot do that. I cannot wake Adam at four a.m. and expect him to come to see his dead brother. I ask the man from the medical examiner's office whether they will be doing the autopsy right away, in half an hour.

The man from the medical examiner's office hesitates. No, he says, that office doesn't open until eight, and they probably won't get to Thor until around ten.

I ask why they need to have Thor back after half an hour.

He says something vague.

I ask whether there is a real reason we can't have Thor longer, or whether that's just procedure for the sake of procedure.

"A little of both," he says.

I stare at him.

I'm glad I didn't have any morphine.

The man from the medical examiner's office relents. "I'll talk to my boss and see what he says."

He returns with his boss a few minutes later. His boss speaks. We can have Thor until Adam and Julia have a chance to come in. They will pick Thor up around ten, when they'll be ready for him.

I SEE Thor. I feel him. I smell him. They have handed him to me in a blanket, and he is heavy in my arms. I rock him and smile at him and sing to him and kiss him and inhale him.

Glenn watches me and cannot understand: I seem happy.

He is right. I am happy, because in this strange new life I have just begun, the life of the mother of a dead child, this is what counts as happiness: I have my baby, I am cradling him and talking to him, and they will not take him away in half an hour, and so I am happy.

2

WHO WAS THOR? OR, *WHAT* WAS THOR? NO. WHO *IS* he? What *is* he?

I don't even know what question to ask.

I do know that all those attempts to be with him were efforts to find out, before it was too late. Holding him and playing with him in the hospital. Visiting him in the funeral home and taking him home for overnight stays over the next days, after his little body had been autopsied and embalmed. Making sure others met him, not just Glenn and I, but also Julia, my family, Glenn's family, our friend Michaela. Taking dozens of pictures, and displaying them, as well as his body in his open casket, at the memorial service.

Or maybe all of those things were just efforts to make sure he was *something*. To make sure he wasn't *nothing*.

What is a baby who dies an hour before he is born?

Is he Thor, the silly name his big brother gave him when I invited him to give whatever was in my still-flat belly a temporary name, as big brother had been "Teal" before he was born and became "Adam"? Or is he Max, the name he was to have had if he had lived, the name of his great-grandfather?

That, too, is the wrong question. He wasn't to have been "Max" if he had lived. He was to have been "Max" if he turned out to be a boy. There was no "if" regarding the question of whether he would live. It never occurred to us that he might not. Our imaginations didn't stretch that far.

How do you make sure your baby who died an hour before he was born is not nothing? Do you do it by creating a biography for him to put on the funeral program? Do you do it by dressing him yourself and rubbing lotion onto his face? Do you do it by buying a plain, pine casket and having his father finish it, by having his big brother paint the lid? Do you do it by making your own temporary grave marker and decorating it with dragonflies, rather than using the generic one offered by the funeral home? Do you do it by hanging a bird feeder at his grave at the edge of the woods, to make sure he has visitors, friends? Do you do it by showing him the rooms in your house and reading to him and telling him stories, so he gathers some experiences, so he has his own unique little life, even if it comes after he died? Do you do it by granting him experiences and preferences and personality from the days before he was born: he disliked flying, but liked swimming?

Do you do it by writing about him?

II

Belle Époque

1

MAYBE I SHOULDN'T START WITH A QUESTION. MAYBE I should start with a statement, something I know.

Before Thor was Thor, Thor was Swimmy.

I named him that because at our first ultrasound, at eleven weeks, he swam around like a maniac. Zip, zip, zip, back and forth across the screen. Then he did a little tumble and thrust his foot forward—the technician gave us a nice printout of his foot. The nurses couldn't help laughing, he was so full of energy, such a goofball. And so, although the reason for the ultrasound was serious—I was forty-five, so there was a real risk of chromosomal abnormalities—and although the procedure involved poking a very long needle through my belly and the wall of my uterus to scrape a bit of tissue from my placenta, Glenn and I were in good cheer.

Glenn didn't know Swimmy, the little fish in the children's book who saves all the other little fish by convincing them to arrange themselves into the shape of a great big fish with him, Swimmy, as the eye. The big fish that had threatened each of them individually suddenly isn't so big anymore, and swims away from the apparently huge fish in fear. This was Glenn's first child, and he had no exposure to kids' books.

But Swimmy was part of my life. Adam had liked the book as a little kid, and when I'd found a Swimmy bumper sticker,

I'd bought it and put it on the car that Adam, years later, painted in psychedelic colors. The bumper sticker was badly faded by now, but you could still make out the school of little fish arranged in the shape of a great big fish, its open mouth surrounding the big fish who no longer looked so big. Below the picture was the word: ORGANIZE.

After the ultrasound, I borrowed the book from the library and read it to Glenn. But we kept the name a secret. Really, we weren't going to give the little critter a name until we knew that everything was OK, and it would take a couple of weeks to get the test results.

Once we found out Swimmy's chromosomes were in order, we told Adam that I was pregnant, and that he could pick out a name, since we'd kind of cheated by naming it ahead of time. Adam had always had naming privileges in our house, though so far those privileges had always applied to pets: first to the hamsters, mice, cats, guinea pigs, kittens, lizards, and snakes Julia and I had gotten while we were still together, then to the two cats I had gotten just weeks before Glenn and I became a couple. It would be a temporary name, we told Adam, since we weren't going to find out the baby's sex until it was born.

Adam immediately had his name: "Thor Level Seventy Dark Mage."

It was exactly the kind of name I would have expected from him. Adam had commuted to junior high on a unicycle, wearing a shocking pink, knee-length, rabbit fur coat that some friends had given him for his fourteenth birthday after he'd admired it in Ragstock (twenty-five bucks!); mismatched, multicolored, striped socks; and a red and black velour mad-hatter hat. Everyone on the east side of town knew the kid riding his unicycle in his pink fur coat, even if they didn't know who he was. In high school, what everyone on the east side of town knew was our car, a clunky old 1995 Nissan Sentra, manual everything, big dent in the right front panel where someone had opened a cab door into it. Everyone knew the car because Adam had painted it in crazy bright colors, a scene of an ocean storm on one side (blowing cloud disguising the dent), bubbles and fields of grass on the other, a sun on the front hood, a demented smiley face on the back, and a multicolored spiral on top, which I didn't fully appreciate until I once peered down on it from the seventeenth floor of a hotel in St. Paul. Whenever we drove, college students would give us the thumbs-up, and little kids would grab their parents' hands and point and wave and jump up and down.

Adam likes attention. But mainly, he likes making art—art of himself, of our car, of the soundscape, of words, of dumpsters, of exterior and basement walls, of every piece of paper he can get his hands on, of his computer screen. He likes when other people make art; he is as fascinated by their creations as he is of his own, but more patient with their imperfections. He thinks highly of himself, but in an easy, relaxed way, as if to say, "Yeah, I'm pretty great, but that doesn't make me anything special, since mainly everyone I know is pretty great, including you." He is crazily charismatic. He is completely gentle.

Adam tended toward ironically bombastic nicknames: a few years earlier he'd named himself "Notorious Milkshake."

But, I now said, "Thor Level Seventy Dark Mage" wouldn't do. We needed a gender-neutral name.

"Thor is not a boy," he came back at me. "Thor is a God."

I left aside the matter of gendered deities and told him, fine, we'll call it "Mage" for short, since that was gender neutral. But "Mage" didn't stick. Mage sounded like Marge, which not only was gendered but also conjured up images of Marge Simpson, blue hair piled up on top of an oversized embryonic head, swimming about and sticking out her foot for the camera. And so Thor Level Seventy Dark Mage became Thor, with the pronoun "it," which worked in our bilingual German-English household. "Baby," "infant," and "child" are all grammatically neutral in German's *der-die-das* system, so sentences like "This is a truly excellent baby—just look at how it showed off its foot for its ultrasound" sound perfectly natural.

Though when I think back on my pregnancy now, I think "he" because after he died we learned he'd been a boy all along.

Thor was ridiculous—how could he not be? A little worm, the size of my pinky, paddling around in amniotic fluid, demanding to be addressed as a god. We had a girl's name and a boy's name picked out for when we finally knew what sex the baby would be, but Thor never became Maggie-Thor or Max-Thor. Thor just remained Thor.

2

"I AM A FERTILITY GODDESS," I TOLD GLENN. "FIRST I get pregnant with a woman, then I get pregnant at forty-five."

"Indeed," Glenn said.

"Yes. If I'd lived my whole adult life with men, and at an earlier time, when they didn't have such good birth control, I'd have six kids and six abortions behind me by now." I'm a historian of women and sexuality, and such people have no illusions about how women used to control their fertility.

"Good thing Julia saved you from that fate," Glenn said.

GLENN AND I had some help. When we decided we wanted to have a kid, I said: "Good, let's go see our doctors to make sure everything's in order, check your sperm count, my hormone levels, that kind of stuff."

"I don't really think that will be necessary," Glenn said. "I did that before Katrin wanted to get pregnant." Katrin was an old friend of Glenn's, with whom he'd shared a long history of sexual tension and a brief romance that remained mainly platonic. By the time she wanted a child, she was with a woman. But Glenn had agreed to help out.

They'd only tried once. Katrin didn't get pregnant. Then Glenn realized he just wasn't comfortable with the idea of fathering a kid he wouldn't help to raise. It had been different for Adam's father. Tony had figured if Julia and I wanted a kid, we should be able to have a kid, and the moment when a lesbian couple wanted to get pregnant was no time for men to suddenly discover that they couldn't possibly father children they weren't prepared to raise. But also: Tony didn't want children of his own. He knew he'd feel no desire to parent the child who was biologically his, though he was glad to be friends with him—after all, he was friends with their mothers. We were happy that Adam would know Tony: no adolescent drama of searching for the missing father.

But Glenn had always wanted kids. The thought of helping to make one who would then live across the ocean—Katrin and Maria lived in Germany—was too much to bear.

"That was years ago! Get checked again. I don't want to go through all the stress of trying to get pregnant—timing sex and everything—and have it not work, and *then* discover there's something we should have found out about ahead of time."

GLENN'S SPERM count, it turned out, was fine. But his sperm motility wasn't. His urologist referred us to the reproductive endocrinology clinic. On our first visit, we saw the cover sheet for our file, which read: "Referring physician: Dr. Moses Wood, Urology. Diagnosis: Unspecified Female Infertility."

Glenn surely knew what was coming on the drive back home: my rant about how the medical profession pins all fertility problems on the woman. With a referral by a *urologist?* A urologist known for his work on male infertility?

Barb, whom I'd been seeing in the Family Practice Clinic for ten years, had run some hormone tests on me and declared I was years away from menopause. I'd already had one baby, the result of exactly two months of trying with Tony. And I figured I had genetics on my side. My mother had managed to get pregnant on every form of birth control in use in the early and midsixties—which, she'd be the first to tell you, had a lot to do with the fact that she wasn't the most reliable user—but still. She hadn't hit menopause till her fifties.

In practice, the doctors were more sensible than our intake sheet. If Glenn had low sperm motility, the thing to do was intrauterine insemination, IUI for short. I took the minimum dose of Clomid to make sure I was ovulating, used an ovulation predictor kit (a.k.a. "pee stick") to see when the egg was about to pop out, and when the pee stick read positive, we went to the clinic. There Glenn "deposited a sample" in the "collection room" (the "masturbatorium" to us), the lab technicians "washed" it (they put it in a solution and then into a centrifuge, which concentrates the perky sperm and leaves behind most of the sluggish ones), and a nurse squirted the washed sperm straight into my uterus with a catheter, saving those lame sperm the effort of swimming through my vagina and cervix to get to my uterus. Glenn got to do his part in a darkened room with a comfy sofa and, if he was so inclined, porn; I did mine on an examining table under bright lights with my feet in stirrups and a speculum hanging out of me; but there you go. It's less uncomfortable than a pap smear.

I told Glenn I imagined his sperm hobbling along with walkers, trying to make their way to my old-lady egg with teased white hair and too much lipstick.

It worked. I got pregnant in late January.

3

JULIA AND I HAD MOVED TO IOWA CITY IN 1999. WHEN you live in Iowa, and most of your friends live on the coasts or in big cities like Chicago, you can wait a long time until any of them deign to visit. Why would they come to Iowa when *of course* you must be dying for an excuse to visit New York or San Francisco?

But every now and then, someone expressed an interest in seeing us in our new habitat. At that point, we'd set into motion a three-stage plan. First, we'd make absolutely sure that they understood the difference between Iowa, Ohio, and Idaho, so they didn't accidentally book a flight to Columbus or Boise. Then, once they'd picked up their rental car at the airport, we'd describe the hilliest possible route to our house— which also happened to be the shortest—to disabuse them of the notion that Iowa was flat. Finally, we'd tell them that once they'd taken that last left onto Ronalds Street, they should look for the house with the white picket fence, apple tree, and front porch swing. That was us.

This was where we'd landed after years of being itinerant academics. I doubled the size of the vegetable garden and tamed the century-old grapevines in the backyard. Julia extended the white picket fence from the front half of the property to the back and, with her brother's help, put in a brick terrace under the pear tree nestled behind the house. Adam declared that his room must be red, and so we painted it red.

I was looking out the back window at our cozy yard one December morning in 2004 when Julia said it, in her gentle German accent:

"We're going to have to separate."

We had been together seventeen years.

We'd both known this was coming for a long time. And we'd both known, without either one of us having said it, that she'd be the one to do it. She was braver than I was about an unknown future. I was more determined to do anything to keep our family intact for Adam.

"Well, there's nothing to discuss then, is there?" I spat. Because she didn't say "I want to separate," which might suggest that what I wanted might also be worth knowing. She just said, "We're going to have to separate."

She'd told me the night before that there was something we needed to talk about, but that we'd let it wait till the morning. I hadn't had any feeling of doom. We always had things we needed to talk about. One of us had run into a roadblock on our research and wanted to bounce some ideas off the other. One of us had some new thoughts about what Adam should do in the summer.

The fact that our relationship had been falling apart for years didn't mean we'd stopped being best friends, political allies, and each other's most important intellectual collaborators. That was why I'd figured we could just keep it together. Really, we had a great relationship. It was just that we weren't lovers anymore. We'd both lost our attraction to women.

She knew last night that she was going to say this this morn-

ing, I thought. *She knew last night that we were going to break up today.*

Last night we'd gone to dinner with our friends Phil and Tina, to the best restaurant in town. Phil and Tina loved to eat well.

That night at dinner, Julia knew we would be breaking up the next day.

Later that day, the day Julia told me, "We're going to have to separate," I went for a walk.

"It's over, it's over, it's over," I said to myself as I walked. The trees were bare and the sky was overcast. I was furious that Julia would interrupt Adam's childhood this way. We'd do the separation in the most delicate way possible, one that didn't involve tense discussions in front of him, one that didn't involve making him choose sides, one that didn't involve making him step into an adult role before his time. But still. He'd led a charmed life. And he knew that our family was rock solid—knew it so deeply that he had never even asked the question: Could something possibly happen to us? Except that it wasn't solid, and he was about to learn that. And when he learned that, he'd have to wonder if he could ever trust his own perception of the world again. If he'd gotten this wrong, how could he be sure of anything?

But there was nothing to be done about it. "We're going to have to separate." It was decided. That chapter of my life was over.

Which meant that the next chapter was about to begin. *Well,* I thought, kicking the leaves along the bricked street that marks the north end of the old part of Iowa City, *time to call that Chinese orphanage.*

I MEANT that figuratively. *Chinese* wasn't the point. What I really thought a few hours after Julia had said that it was over, was: *Now I can see about having that second kid that I always wanted and Julia didn't.*

That spring I started the process of getting licensed as a foster parent. Orientation, training, interviews with social workers, medical forms, financial information, criminal record checks, letters of reference. It took a year.

A few weeks after I was licensed, Glenn and I became a couple, and a few months after that—around the same time Glenn got his foster license—we decided to try to have a kid of our own. And so we hesitated when the social workers called us with possible placements.

It was Julia who had it figured out. "As soon as you take a placement," she said, "you'll get pregnant."

That wasn't the reason I said "yes" when the call for Rae-Rae and Kiki came. I said "yes" because I was boiling at the newspaper coverage of the incident that had resulted in the kids' removal from their home—and especially at the online comments to the story, which by and large demanded compulsory sterilization of the mother. The incident seemed at most ambiguous to me.

"That does it," I said to Glenn. "All these kids need is to land in the hands of one of those judgmental assholes. We're taking them."

Kiki was a tomboyish six-year-old who hated to get up in the morning. Nine-year-old Rae-Rae stuck out her hip and rolled her eyes whenever I said something stupid, laughing all the while to let me know she was just messing around. Five days after they came to us, I discovered I was pregnant. Six weeks later, they were back home—near record time for the child welfare system. Even the judges and social workers could tell, once they looked just a little bit closer, that Rae-Rae and Kiki's home situation was fine.

We stayed in touch—we'd become friendly with their mother and her three younger kids, who had been placed in a different home. A few days after the stillbirth, Rae-Rae phoned from Chicago, where they now lived. She read me a letter she'd written, full of her ideas for names for the baby. She didn't know that Thor had already been born and had already died, and I didn't tell her. She thought we could name the baby "Lynisia" if it was a girl, because it sounded like "Lisa" but wasn't quite the same so people wouldn't mix us up. Or "Glendina," if we wanted to name it after Glenn. If it was a boy, maybe "Kitanje," because she liked how that sounded. She didn't know if she'd be able to send the letter, because she also had lots of presents for the baby, and her mother said the postage might be too expensive. That's why she'd called to read it to me. She called a few days later to see if the baby was there yet, and I still didn't tell her. Finally, I called her mother during school hours, so she could pass on the news to the kids—it seemed like something they should hear from her.

The next time I talked to Rae-Rae, I asked her to send me the letter. I had so few *things* from Thor's little life, especially things that could let me imagine that he had a relationship to other people, not just me and Glenn. But she had lost it, and now I don't even know if I'm remembering the names she'd picked out right.

4

GLENN AND I HAD BECOME A COUPLE NEARLY TWO years before we took in Rae-Rae and Kiki. The semester was over—we both taught at the university—and the first months of our relationship were charmed by the summer. One Saturday, early on, we took a long bike ride. It wasn't hot yet—just perfect biking weather, clear and still. I pumped my legs hard, liberated by the open road to bear ahead, not like my stop-and-go commute in the city. My lungs were a little raw from a recent cold, and every breath scratched its way in, but I knew by the time we got to the little town of Hills, I'd have forgotten all about it. By then, I'd be focusing on my rear, which was unaccustomed to spending more than a few minutes at a time on a bike seat. This was my first real ride of the season.

We biked along the river for a while, shaded by trees, and then emerged onto the open road: past the softball fields, past the ugly new housing development going in south of town, past the plant nursery, and onto a long, straight stretch with not much other than corn and soy fields and the occasional house on either side. The seedlings were just a couple of inches high, and the long rows of them created delicate, green stripes against the raw, brown earth.

"So, Doris wanted to set me up with Rosemary," he said, "but that didn't really go anywhere." Doris was like that, attentive to the fact that Iowa City was a hard place to be single, wanting to make sure everyone was happy.

I wasn't surprised. Rosemary had come to Iowa City a few years earlier, recently divorced; of course Doris had tried to set them up. Doris was probably thinking that Rosemary and Glenn shared some academic interests, but actually, they were completely different types. Rosemary had done ten years in the Navy and was seriously athletic; she came from the South and always felt a little awkward around the northern academics who surrounded her.

"Actually, Rosemary mentioned to me that Doris had tried to fix you up," I said.

"Really!" Glenn glanced sideways at me for just a minute before returning his eyes to the road. Glenn looks pretty professorial—balding and a little jowly, though he's a couple of years younger than I am—but on a bike what you notice is his long torso and the bend of his hips leading to legs shaded by even, black hair. "What did she say?"

"Oh, the same thing you said, pretty much. She thinks Doris is very sweet, but nothing much was going to come of it."

"Did she say why?" Heh heh. Glenn wanted to know what Rosemary thought of him.

"She found you 'fussy.'" I snuck a sideways look to see his reaction. His brow wrinkled.

"Fussy?! What does she mean by that? When did she say I was *fussy*?"

"I don't know. She didn't point to any particular episode."

"Maybe she's thinking of this one time . . . this must be it . . . medieval studies had a guest lecturer, and I hosted a reception at my house; Rosemary was there, and I know I was very careful to go around and ask everyone if they wanted another drink, make sure the snacks circulated . . . maybe she thought that was fussy."

"Hm, maybe, I don't know," I said.

"But I wanted to be a good host! Maybe I was being too attentive?" His eyes pinched with concern. "You know how tight my living room is! I was having to say 'excuse me' a lot to make sure to circulate to everyone there . . . maybe I should have left everyone to their own devices. I don't know, though— I wanted to be a good host!"

"Honestly, I don't know. She never mentioned that party to me."

"So, what could it have been? What does 'fussy' mean?"

"I asked her that too. She said, 'Not masculine enough.'"

Way to add fat to the fire! I thought, jolting to my senses. I tried to think of some sort of save.

But it wasn't necessary.

Glenn's face relaxed. "Oh, is that all!" He broke into a smile. "Not masculine enough? I can embrace that!" He raised his chin and looked forward as if a bright future had suddenly revealed itself to him, and if he just kept pedaling, he'd get there soon.

THERE IS a term for people like Glenn: a lesbian trapped in a man's body. I was just the latest in a long string of girlfriends (and one wife) who either had been involved with women before connecting with him, or were on their way to women after separating from him.

Who keeps falling in love with lesbians but another lesbian?

GLENN WAS emerging from what I came to think of as his lonely years. He more neutrally called them his bachelor years. In college he fell in love with all things German, and he arranged to study abroad his senior year so he could stay in Germany after graduation. He lived in Freiburg for three years, and towards the end of his time there, he got involved with Dorothee, a law student. He went to Texas to start graduate school, but he always kept one foot in Germany, trying to keep the relationship going. He spent as much time as he could in Germany, and Dorothee finally agreed to spend a year in Texas.

They got married. For Dorothee, the marriage was an uncomfortable compromise. She bristled at the identity of a wife; she had a troubled relationship with her mother and feared following in her footsteps. But it made sense to get a green card, and she and Glenn were together anyway. For Glenn, the demands of the INS sped up what he'd hoped would come one way or another, though marriage was less important to him than permanence.

Dorothee didn't like Texas, didn't like America, wondered what she was supposed to do with a German law degree in the States, and returned with relief to Germany. Glenn considered following her there and teaching English at community colleges, but then he got a tenure-track job and discovered he wasn't prepared to give up his career for a woman who seemed ambivalent about the relationship. A move to Iowa was out of the question for Dorothee.

They broke up, but it didn't really sink in for Glenn. During their entire relationship, they'd been apart more than they'd been together, and nothing changed in his daily life. After three and a half years in Iowa, he spent a semester in Germany, working on a book, but also trying to clarify where he and Dorothee stood. For Dorothee, it was perfectly clear where they stood. Only after he returned to Iowa did he begin the process of separating emotionally from her. He was now nearing tenure, and he'd been in a relationship that had involved more time apart than together since before he'd begun grad school.

What came then was a series of dead-end relationships. A woman who declared that she needed more drama than Glenn could provide. A woman who provided all the drama anyone could ever want by turning into a stalker after Glenn broke up with her. A woman whose heart just wasn't in it. A woman whose enjoyment of Glenn's company couldn't withstand the serious turn of an unwanted pregnancy. And so on. The years rolled by—he turned thirty-five, thirty-eight, forty, forty-two—and Glenn, who always had wanted children, saw his hopes for a family dwindle.

And no intellectual community sprang up to fill the gap. Graduate school had been a world of intense camaraderie among young people who shared a fascination for subjects that very few people understood. But that's not what working academia was like, at least not his corner of it. The German department had a troubled history, with the kind of battles that—as an observer of academia once put it—could be so bitter only because the stakes were so low. Glenn tried to make peace among the factions, not understanding what every historian knows: diplomacy can only succeed if the warring parties are fundamentally interested in peace. He learned to fear for his job.

Tenure was a victory, but it was also sobering. He would

almost surely spend the rest of his career in Iowa City, where he had no partner, no family, and colleagues who kept him apprehensive. As the years went on, the department grew more peaceful, but in the meantime, German was declining as a discipline. Really, the days were long gone when mastery of Goethe and Schiller was required to qualify one as an educated person—and Glenn's specialty was far more rarified than Goethe and Schiller. Glenn loved his work, but he knew that when he and the three other American specialists in medieval and early modern German theater retired, they could turn off the lights and close the door. They would not be replaced. The field to which he'd dedicated his career would simply go extinct in North America.

It was a depressing life. Glenn bought a little house, which he shared with two kittens named Fee Fi and Fo Fum. He kept looking for a relationship that would work, kept trying to convince himself his work was worth doing, kept hoping his department would someday turn into a community.

Which is why he could scarcely believe his luck when I turned from a casual acquaintance to a lover. But then, I could hardly believe my luck either.

LATER DURING that first summer of our relationship, Glenn and I went to Lake Okoboji, in the northwest part of the state, near South Dakota. The travel literature refers to the area as "Iowa's Great Lakes." Lake Okoboji has a very old amusement park, only a couple of square blocks, with an eighty-year-old roller coaster whose supports are made entirely of wood. I learned there that you don't need a particularly high or fast roller coaster to get the living daylights scared out of you on an amusement park ride. All you have to do is look at the warped rails ahead of you as you careen around a curve and remember that the roller coaster you're riding is eighty years old.

The day we drove out to Lake Okoboji was gorgeous: sunny, clear, not too hot. We were both in a wonderful mood, freshly in love and taking a weekend off. Somewhere along the way, we pulled over—I don't remember why. It's possible I was driving and I pulled over for the sole purpose of kissing him. Or perhaps we were switching drivers, and I grabbed him as we passed by the back of the car on our way to swap seats. In any case, our hearts were overflowing, and we kissed and leaned our foreheads against each others' in the sunlight, touching and smelling and tasting each other, next to a soybean field with plants now knee-high, across the street from a little service station.

Julia and I wouldn't have done that. It's not that I would have refrained from kissing her in public when I was bursting with love. Rather, I would have refrained from bursting with love in a way that made it necessary to kiss her, right then and there, wherever we may have been and whoever may have seen us. I'd learned the habit of self-censorship—not of my actions or words, but of my feelings.

Maybe only people who go from same-sex relationships— the adult, committed kind; the kind that involve raising a child together; the kind that involve trying to find two academic jobs together and, in the meantime, hoping the place that employs one of you has benefits for same-sex partners; the kind that involve fighting the INS because one of you needs a Green Card and you can't get married—maybe only people who move from those kinds of relationships to straight relationships can truly understand the meaning of heterosexual privilege, because it goes so far beyond employment benefits and marriage and the INS. I didn't get involved with a man because I wanted to enjoy heterosexual privilege, and it was uncomfortable for me, once I was with Glenn, not to have my very presence in a room be a challenge to those around me. But no matter how many perks of straight life I declined—not getting married, not identifying the sex of my "partner" in conversations with strangers—it was impossible not to enjoy the freedom of emotion. At the age of forty-five, for the first time in my life, my heart could scream in a way that made it necessary for me to grab my beloved and kiss him next to a soybean field across the street from a little service station, not far from the South Dakota border.

5

NOW IT WAS SPRING, ALMOST TWO YEARS LATER, AND we were going to have a baby.

The first person to know, aside from Glenn and me, was Barb. I'd been seeing her for ten years in the Family Practice Clinic at the university hospital. My annual physical happened to be the day after I took the home pregnancy test.

"How are you doing?" Barb asked as soon as she walked into the examining room.

"I'm pregnant."

"Really! That's great, wonderful!" She knew we'd been trying. "Let me get a test, we'll confirm it."

Barb is my age, maybe just a little older. She has graying, curly hair and a face that sometimes looks slightly afraid when she's listening closely.

"Yep, you're pregnant!" Barb said, waving the pee stick in the air as she came back into the room, then considerately holding it at arm's length as she gave me a hug.

"So let's talk about prenatal care," she said as she sat down. "Where do you want to get it?"

"What are my options? Last time I worked with a midwives' practice, and it was great. But that was sixteen years ago, and in Berlin. I know the situation for midwives is different here."

"It is. There's a midwives' practice in the hospital, though, part of the OB-GYN clinic. That might be good for you. Your other options are to go with an OB-GYN, but of course they tend to be high tech. Lots of interventions, probably not what you're looking for, unless there are complications, in which case you'll definitely need to see them. We also see prenatal patients here in Family Care, but because of your age I'm not sure I'd be comfortable with that."

"So what's your impression of the midwives' practice? Is there anyone in particular there you recommend?"

"I think they're all good. I'm pretty sure you'd see all of them—at least, you'd have the option of doing that, and I'd recommend it, since any one of them can be on duty when you actually give birth."

"OK, I'll make an appointment. Anything I should be thinking about in the meantime?"

She gave me the long list of dos and don'ts, mainly don'ts. No alcohol, no raw meat or fish, no cold cuts, no soft cheeses, etc. "You know, all these rules. No one follows them all, but some of them are pretty critical. You really don't want a parasite. Just stay healthy. Eat right. Exercise. Don't drink." She shrugged and smiled. "You've got the body of someone ten years younger. You take care of yourself. Just use your common sense."

IT WAS true: I was outrageously healthy. Still, we had to cross one last hurdle before we could breathe easy.

I was *old*. I was going to be forty-six when I delivered. How old is that? So old that the charts predicting the likelihood of a baby with Down syndrome didn't even cover me. They stopped at forty-five. At that point, the risk is roughly one in ten, though there was enough variance from one chart to the next that you had to wonder if there was reliable data for women that old, or if the doctors were just giving a ballpark figure.

The chart I carried from the receptionist to my first prenatal appointment with the midwives bore the dark red stamp "AMA," for "advanced maternal age." The first time I saw the stamp, I was torn between annoyance at the tendency to pathologize middle age among women and the desire for a label that did a better job showing how special I was. AMA is for any pregnant woman over thirty-five—they're a dime a dozen! I started referring to my "geriatric pregnancy" instead.

I liked the attitude of the midwives at OB-GYN. They only worked with low-risk patients, and as they explained, my age didn't make me high risk. My age put me at increased risk for certain conditions, which in turn would make for a high-risk pregnancy, but we could test for those conditions. If I didn't have any of them—obesity, high blood pressure, gestational diabetes, chromosomal abnormalities—then I was low risk. My blood pressure was so low that years ago I'd stopped trying to give blood—I was always turned away because of low blood pressure. (They're afraid you might faint, though I never did.) Obesity, no. Gestational diabetes, no. Smoking, drinking, cocaine, no. All that remained was the chromosomal testing. But I tended to feel lucky about such things. Nine out of ten was still very good odds. I'd gotten into colleges and grad schools, won grants and jobs, that were much more competitive than that.

Still, I was going to do my homework. The fact was, we could have a dilemma on our hands. But a big part of the reason I threw myself into researching Down syndrome is that this was exactly the kind of intellectual and ethical problem that had led me to become a historian of women and sexuality in the first place. Abortion rights meets disability rights meets eugenics. Yes, I needed to know more about Down syndrome and what parenting a Down syndrome child involved, but I also just liked grappling with this kind of stuff.

I spent a couple of days researching Down syndrome online. Sites for parents and professionals dealing with Down syndrome kids had good information about the condition. I hadn't known anything about the various physical ailments that often accompany the mental disability. If you looked hard, you could learn about the range of mental abilities, though the fact that you had to look hard was telling: how to talk about the true range of disability was a sore point in this community. Some of the sites gave over most of their space to inspiring high-functioning cases. Others complained that sites like these made the vast majority of parents, whose kids would never be independent, feel completely inadequate and frustrated at the lack of attention to their needs. One thing was crystal clear: the Down syndrome sites didn't want to deal with people who were deciding whether to abort a fetus with chromosomal abnormalities. Some were screamingly antiabortion, because in this context abortion was clearly about declaring disabled kids— *their* kids—undesirable. Most banned the A-word entirely in the interest of keeping peace on their discussion boards.

And so I went where all intellectual types go when they're

pondering this kind of stuff: to Michael Berube. Berube is a culture studies big shot who has a child with Down syndrome. He wrote a book about his child; about the medical, social, and political issues swirling around Down syndrome; about eugenics and abortion rights; about services for people with disabilities and information made available to parents trying to decide whether to terminate a pregnancy. He doesn't leave you with any clear answers, but that was fine with me. I wasn't looking for someone to tell me what to do. I was looking for a serious discussion. I checked out his book from the university library.

Of course, I really wanted to have the serious discussion with Glenn, and that meant he needed to read up too. Otherwise, our discussions would take the form of me educating him about what I'd read, and that would be no discussion at all. But Glenn didn't feel the need to pore through academic tomes on the subject, because he wasn't going to tie himself up in knots about eugenics. He hadn't spent years of his life researching Nazi reproductive politics, as I had. He hadn't had a seventeen-year-long relationship with someone like Julia who wrote about eugenic sterilization in the United States. He had papers to grade, which he did, in bed, as I read Michael Berube's book.

It was very aggravating not being able to turn every possible angle of this problem inside out with Glenn because he refused to do his homework. I'd already done the pre-sorting for him. If he wanted to look at a website or two, I could tell him which ones were best—in fact, I'd sent him the links. He didn't need to wade through the piles of books available on Down syndrome, because I'd already selected the one that would be most important for us, and I'd brought it home from the library.

I kept asking him when he was finally going to start reading The Book. I reminded him of just how little time we'd have to decide once we had the test results, and had he forgotten that the test was scheduled for *next week*, and not to put too fine a point on it, but he did read somewhat slower than I did and would need a little extra time—was he keeping all of this in mind?

Glenn remained unflappable. He didn't want to have a child with Down syndrome. But in the end, it was my decision. He wasn't going to pressure me into an abortion, just like he hadn't pressured a former girlfriend out of an abortion though he'd really wanted the kid. When he said he didn't want a baby with Down syndrome, he wasn't saying we couldn't or shouldn't have one—he was just expressing his preference. Zen Glenn would deal with whatever life brought his way. And although I didn't want it to be *my* decision—I wanted him to take equal responsibility for it—the fact was, I didn't get too worked up because really, I knew, the baby wasn't going to have Down syndrome anyway. Nine out of ten was very good odds.

After we had the test, a procedure that required the ultrasound that gave us our first glimpse of Swimmy and Swimmy's foot, we waited for the test results. One day, we arrived home to find the light blinking on our answering machine, and we listened to a nurse's voice tell us the baby had all its chromosomes in order. If we'd gotten a message saying the results were in and we should call, we knew, the news would be bad. They'd leave good news, but not bad, on an answering machine.

Swimmy was fine, Swimmy was fine, Swimmy was fine.

I looked up at Glenn and grinned. He grabbed my hand and swung me about.

"I knew it!" I said.

"How did you know it?"

I twirled away from him, leaving our arms stretched high toward each other, linked at the fingertips a moment, and then I detached mine and danced away, waving over my shoulder.

"Bad things don't happen to me!"

I winked, stuck out my tongue, and waltzed into the kitchen to make some dinner.

6

I LEARNED THAT THERE WAS A MIDWIFE PERFORMING
home births legally in Iowa.

I'd been seeing the nurse-midwives in the hospital ever
since Barb recommended them. Since I was low risk, I could
get my prenatal care from them and have a midwife attend my
labor. But this was still a hospital. An obstetrician I'd never
met would show up at the last minute to supervise the actual
delivery. I would be in a hospital room, with nurses and physicians' assistants and interns wandering in and out through my
labor and delivery, taking measurements, paying close attention to the machines they knew so much better than they knew
me, working from the assumption that their job would involve
some injection, *some* pill, *some* cut. Once they gave that first
injection or pill, the chances of further interventions would
rise dramatically. Each intervention would bring its own risks
as the baby might respond badly to medication intended for
me, or as I might become less able to do my part, culminat-
ing with a good chance of an emergency C-section and all its
consequences: longer recovery time for me, lower likelihood
of successful breastfeeding, loss of the benefits for the baby
that go with breastfeeding, and so on and so forth, never mind
the various risks associated with any surgery like infection or
side-effects of anesthesia. Once the baby was born, the pedi-

atric staff would take over. They would cut the umbilical cord immediately instead of letting the baby start to breathe on its own. They would whisk it to a warming table rather than letting it stay warm on my body. NICU was right down the hall, so if there was any problem, the baby would go straight there. Once it was in NICU, it wouldn't be released until it had surpassed its birth weight, even though all babies lose weight their first few days. The midwives cringed a little when they told me this. There was some tension between pediatrics and OB-GYN, they said, because OB-GYN found pediatrics a little too aggressive. But once the baby is there, the baby is pediatrics' patient, not theirs. The mother is their patient.

I asked what the hospital's C-section rate was. The midwife said, "Thirty, thirty-five percent."

I asked if that wasn't a little high.

"We're the most advanced hospital statewide. So we get all the high-risk patients."

I asked what the C-section rate was for the midwives' practice.

The midwife looked sheepishly at me. "Fifteen percent."

"But your patients are all low risk." The World Health Organization has said that a C-section rate of 10 to 15 percent for *all* births would represent the best medical practice: doing C-sections when they're necessary, but only then.

She nodded, and sighed. "We're still in a hospital," she said. "We're still in an OB-GYN culture."

I'D HAD Adam in an independent midwives' practice in Berlin. That was in 1991. You had to see an obstetrician a few times for prenatal care—there were many obstetricians who knew the midwives' clinic and worked gladly with their patients. And you had to choose a backup hospital in case things got complicated or you decided you wanted medication. But if that didn't happen, the birth took place in the birthing center and was simply attended by the midwife.

I'd liked the birthing center, liked the fact that several midwives worked together and that there was a special place for delivery. We'd had the option of a home birth with the midwives' practice, but Julia and I had lived on a fifth-floor walkup with no bathtub, only a shower, and so we'd thought going to the center for the birth would be nice. But medically speaking, a birth attended by a midwife in an independent midwifery clinic is the same as a home birth attended by a midwife. It's just a different building.

A VOCABULARY lesson:

"Direct-entry midwives" enter midwifery directly, without getting a nursing degree. They typically learn their trade by apprenticing with experienced midwives, and they specialize in out-of-hospital prenatal care, delivery, and postpartum care for low-risk patients. Sometimes they're derogatorily called "lay midwives." A slim majority of states credential direct-entry midwives who have undergone an approved course of training and a battery of examinations. Then they're called certified professional midwives, or CPMs. But Iowa does not license CPMs, and so its direct-entry midwives practice illegally.

Do you think if the state doesn't license CPMs, then there won't be midwives performing home births? Do you think all those Amish women are going to traipse to the hospital and allow themselves to be hooked up to machines?

Iowa, like all states, has nurse-midwives, who get special training in midwifery as part of their nursing education. They're called certified nurse-midwives, or CNMs. Nurse-midwives can legally attend out-of-hospital births, but since they're trained in hospitals, they tend only to feel comfortable doing hospital births, and so they work in hospitals. In some countries, nurse-midwives live in a culture less suspicious of out-of-hospital births, and so they more easily take up that line of work. That's how it was in Berlin—the midwives' center was staffed by nurse-midwives.

Until 2008, you had two choices in Iowa: hospital birth, or home birth attended by a direct-entry midwife practicing illegally. I knew a lot of those direct-entry midwives were good at what they did. I thought they were brave, risking their careers and even the possibility of jail in order to provide a service that could be provided safely—and whose safety would only increase with legalization, since then there could be some standardization of practice and checks on practitioners who did a poor job.

But I'm a goody-two-shoes. I was squeamish about going the illegal route. Besides, there were practical questions. How can you check the record of midwives practicing illegally to see which are good and which have a history of problems? What if there were a complication—would a midwife practicing illegally stick around to fill the hospital staff in on my condition, or would that be too risky for her? I gritted my teeth and worked with the nurse-midwives in the hospital, who believed in minimizing intervention but had a fifteen percent C-section rate with their uniformly low-risk patients.

Then I learned about Deirdre. Deirdre had practiced as a

direct-entry midwife for many years. Then she had decided to get her nursing degree and become a certified nurse midwife. Not so she could work in the hospital, but so she could attend home births legally. When I met her, she had been licensed less than a year but had practiced for over twenty, with no "bad outcomes." That means no delivery-related disabilities or deaths. She lived two blocks away from Glenn and me.

WE MET Deirdre for the first time in August. Her voice boomed as she opened the door to her home.

"Hello, hello! Come on in!"

Deirdre was a common-sense Midwesterner. She was tall with shoulder-length brown hair, carried her little bit of extra weight comfortably, and squinted when she laughed, which she did frequently and heartily. Even the little stud on her left nostril looked corn fed.

"Well, you must be Lisa and Glenn! Come on, sit down, wherever is comfortable for you," she said, sweeping her arm across the living room. Two white sofas from the consignment shop nestled at right angles under the windows. A tiny kitten with very long hair hopped from one of the sofas up to the windowsill and back down again. "Don't mind her," Deirdre said. "She's just an attention hog. Toss her off if you like."

Glenn and I sat down, and Glenn scratched the kitten behind her ears. Deirdre sat on the other sofa and leaned forward, hands folded on her lap. "So," she said, "let's talk."

"Well," I said, "I'm pregnant." I nodded down at my belly, which protruded halfway to my knees.

"Are you now?" Deirdre said.

"Yep. So, here are the basics. I'm forty-six, due October 30.

Easy pregnancy so far. This is my second kid—I have a six-teen-year-old. He was born out-of-hospital in Berlin, full term, uncomplicated delivery."

"And you've been getting regular prenatal care?"

"Yes, with the midwives at the hospital. But I wanted to look into the possibility of a home birth."

"All right," Deirdre said. "Let me tell you a little about how I work. We can do prenatal visits here or at your place—your choice. We'd do the regular schedule of visits—monthly till your last month, then biweekly and more frequently toward the end if we need to. If you go postdate, I see you every other day, but that's looking ahead."

"I'll say."

"A lot of the prenatal visits are really about getting to know each other. We'll talk about what kind of birth you want, what your options are. I'll support you whatever you want to do."

"What are the choices?"

"Well, in terms of who will be there, for example, if you want to have family, friends there, that's fine. But also in terms of the birth itself—some people want to use the aqua doula, some don't—"

"You bring an aqua doula?" I perked up. For me, this was the promise of a vastly less painful labor and delivery, an enor-mous point in favor of a home birth. Even in preparing for Adam's birth, I'd liked the idea of being in warm water while I was laboring. One of the reasons we'd chosen the birthing center over a home birth was that our apartment had only a shower. In the end, we'd gotten to the birthing center too late to use their tub. An aqua doula was even better than a tub because it was bigger: you could actually have the baby in the water. When my father heard about this he asked, giggling a little because he knew the answer had to be "no" or they wouldn't do it, but wanting to be reassured anyway: "The baby won't drown?" No, I explained, the baby doesn't breathe the second it's out since the umbilical cord keeps providing oxygen, just as it's been doing all along, and the baby floats to the top right away. By the time its lungs take over it's above the water.

"You said on the phone you'd been talking to doulas?" Deirdre asked.

"That's right."

"Well, normally I hire a doula—I have a couple that I regularly work with and they know my practice well—but if you have someone you like, we can make arrangements for her to do it."

"No, we really haven't found anyone yet," I said. I liked the idea that she would arrange for a doula. In Berlin, it had been just me, Julia, and the midwife. That had been fine, but I was a little worried that Glenn might not be comfortable with the whole process and might need some support.

"What questions do you have for me?" she asked.

"Tell us a little about your background, how long you've been doing this, that sort of thing."

"Well," Deirdre nodded. "I've been delivering babies twenty-three years. I came up the apprentice way—learned on the job, first as a doula and an assistant. Seven years ago I started work on my nursing degree. I went to school part time, so it took awhile. I got my license last spring, so I opened my practice as a CNM then. Solo practice."

"So if you work on your own, what happens if there are two births at the same time?"

"I try to avoid that." Deirdre pushed her hair back with her hand. "I only take clients with due dates far enough apart so there's some breathing room. You're due late October, and I can only consider you because I don't have anyone past mid-October or in November yet. But in theory it can happen—sometimes babies are off-schedule. Then you have a choice. I can make an arrangement with another midwife, someone whose work I know, who can step in. Or if you'd rather, you can opt for the hospital at that point."

I nodded. Glenn looked at the pad of paper on his lap. A couple of days earlier, he'd talked to his cousin Isabel, a midwife, on the phone. She'd done both hospital and out-of-hospital births and loved the idea of a home birth for us—assuming I was low risk—and she'd suggested some questions for us to ask Deirdre.

"So, I do have some questions," Glenn said.

"Fire away," said Deirdre.

"So, just as background, my cousin is a midwife . . . "

"Oh, wonderful!" Deirdre straightened up and smiled broadly.

"Yes, so she suggested I ask about resuscitations, whether you've ever done them?"

"Yes sir. It's part of the job."

"And you carry oxygen with you?"

"Right, a portable oxygen tank, and a lot of other equipment, everything comes with me."

"And I suppose I wanted to know . . . what happens in cases where there's a real emergency, something like a shoulder dystocia?" Glenn had been reading about delivery emergencies.

"There are manipulations a skilled midwife can do to position the woman optimally and release the posterior shoulder; I've done them. But it's a dangerous complication. We make a plan ahead of time in case a hospital transfer is necessary. You tell me what hospital you'll want to go to. Sometimes there's a transfer because Mom gets exhausted or wants something like an epidural that I can't give. That's fine. But occasionally there is the emergency transfer."

Glenn nodded.

"But really, the whole sudden emergency thing, where everything turns around in a minute, that's for TV dramas. In real life, if something's wrong, you know it ahead of time, or you know it early in labor. It happens in, oh, 10 percent of the cases. I've done transfers to both hospitals in town; they know me at both places. I stay with you if you want, to help out or just provide support, and also so I can give the doctors there whatever medical information they need. Some midwives will just drop you off and leave you—they're in a different position than I'm in; they're worried about getting in trouble. I didn't do that even before I was licensed. You don't just drop off a patient in the middle of labor."

"But people are sometimes transferred during labor?" Glenn asked, a little alarmed.

"That's how it was at the midwives' practice in Berlin, too," I told him. With Glenn, if the Germans do it, it's a little more reassuring. "We all had to have a backup hospital in case something came up. The difference is that here the hospitals are five minutes away, while in Berlin they could be halfway across the city."

"Ri-ight," Glenn nodded, scribbling notes.

"I wanted to ask about postpartum support," I said.

"Oh yes," Deirdre said, "I do that as well. I'll come by and do the baby's first couple of exams, check in on you, make sure everything's healing the way it should, if we had to do an episiotomy or anything like that."

"How about nursing support?" This was a big worry of mine. I'd had trouble nursing Adam, and wished I'd had more help at the time.

"We start that right away, after the birth. But yes, we can talk about that on postpartum visits too. I'll take a look at how you're doing and make suggestions. And I can also connect you with lactation consultants if you need more help. There are a lot of people around; both hospitals have lactation groups."

We asked more questions; Deirdre gave more answers. She was reassuring, humorous, professional. As we walked home, I could barely hold myself back from skipping. We still had more research to do. We'd call Deirdre's references and read the packet of information she'd given us. I'd talk to Barb at Family Practice and to the midwives I'd been seeing at the hospital. Glenn would check in again with Isabel. But now at least we had options, and I felt an enormous wave of relief. Unless there turned out to be some reason why I shouldn't work with Deirdre, then I could have an out-of-hospital birth. Just like with Adam.

7

WHEN PEOPLE ASKED ME WHY I CHOSE HOME BIRTH,
I usually told them about my experience with Adam, explained
the high rate of unnecessary interventions in hospitals and the
risks associated with them, and so on.

But what I thought to myself was much simpler: I chose
a home birth because I believe in evidence-based medicine.
Because I believe in scientific method.

IN MY senior year of college I had a rare phase of spiritual seeking. I'd done most of my spiritual seeking in secret: it mainly
involved reading books and didn't require anything like church
visits that might call attention to me. But this time I was taking
a self-designed course in feminist theology for winter term, and
my mother knew enough to ask what my winter term project
was.

I was home for Christmas break. We sat at the white formica kitchen table, chipped around the edges, in a kitchen
out of the 1970s: dark stained cabinets of plywood, formica
countertops with gold glitter (perhaps to hide dirt), linoleum
flooring with an indeterminate blue-yellow-white squiggly pat-
tern (definitely to hide dirt), and the best part: lemon-yellow,
plastic-paneled walls (easy to wipe down! No smudgy finger-
prints!). The wall was plastered with comic strips clipped from

the newspaper, kids' concert programs, postcards, and family pictures. We sat on chairs whose seats we had once pried off in order to tear away the old, torn vinyl and staple on new dark brown vinyl. A tea cart stood under the window, holding newspapers (bottom shelf), condiments and napkins (middle shelf), and a toaster oven and drip coffee pot (top shelf). This was the site of nearly all important family discussions.

My mother couldn't fathom that I was giving any sort of theology the time of day.

"Do you *believe* any of this stuff?" She leaned forward, dyed-black hair falling around her face, eyes incredulous.

"I don't know . . . I just wanted to read about it." I looked down vaguely, avoiding her gaze.

"Well, what *do* you believe?"

"I don't know," I shrugged defensively. "Nothing! I just feel like it's good to know something about it."

My mother cut me off with a wave of the hand.

"Well, *we* believe in the scientific method," she said, reminding me that not one but two very smart people had already determined that the subject didn't warrant much further thought. "We" meant my father as well as her.

Actually, both of my parents had a much more complicated relationship to religion than I had. My mother had come from a long line of Baptist missionaries and preachers; she'd been born while her parents were on a mission in Burma. Her sister had married a minister. My father had grown up Jewish, fled Nazi Germany without his parents when he was not yet nine years old, and become orthodox as a teenager. Then, in college—she was a botany major, he majored in chemistry— both of them had abandoned religion. My father left it once and for all, but my mother continued to struggle. She missed the community and sense of ethical purpose with which she'd grown up. She replaced it with a lot of secular volunteer work, but she also periodically approached a church or a minister, only to throw up her hands in exasperation when it turned out that said church or minister believed in things she considered patently ridiculous, like a virgin birth. She once said that miracles were easier to stomach the farther back in time they were. Thus Christians were less crazy than Mormons, and Jews less crazy than Christians. Maybe that was why she'd been able to convert to Judaism before marrying my father. It had been a hopeful move, but the Judaism hadn't stuck either.

My mother had sacrificed a lot in losing faith due to her belief in science. Perhaps that helps to explain the virulence with which she rejected any hint of faith on her children's part. She needn't have worried. Her children, too, believed in the scientific method.

AN EARLIER scene at the kitchen table. I'm in grade school—perhaps fourth or fifth grade. The old, scarred vinyl is still on the chairs. The drip coffee pot is not there yet: instead, an ancient percolator sits next to the toaster oven. It's set to a timer to start it boiling early in the morning. My bedroom is right above the kitchen, and sometimes the percolator's whining and harrumphing enters my dreams and I believe I have composed an ethereal, mystical music the likes of which no one has ever heard. I am a musical genius! I'm disappointed when I wake up and discover it's just the coffee pot.

I thrust my thumb out at my father, who is drinking his

coffee with two tablets of saccharine. I show him the bump on my thumb.

Behind his glasses, my father wrinkles his brow. You can see the wrinkles go way back, because he's almost completely bald. In the summer, he knots the four corners of a handkerchief and pops it onto his head—an instant hat, to protect from sunburn. My brother and sister and I find it funny that he is bald, but embarrassing when he wears his handkerchief on his head.

He takes my thumb, turns it over, and examines it carefully. I twirl my braid with my other hand.

"Hmmm," he says ominously. "Looks like cancer! We'd better operate."

I giggle. I know better than that. It's just a little bump. But *some* people, I know, get worked up over every little thing. *Some* people think they have to run to the doctor every time they have the sniffles, or an ache in their knee, or a bump on their thumb. *Some* people will be dissatisfied if the doctor just says those things will go away in a few days if you leave them alone, we don't need to do anything. *Some* people will feel like they must get a pill or a bandage or an operation.

But my Dad's a doctor, and my brother, sister, and I are in on the secret. Doctors might try to make you believe they're gods, but they can't do everything. Sometimes you don't even need a doctor—in fact, if you're basically healthy, *most* of the time you don't need a doctor. Often you're better off without doctors, because they might prescribe something or start some treatment that isn't necessary, just to cover themselves in case of a lawsuit, or because they take pride in doing things no one else can do, or because they think you'll go away more satisfied if they "do something," even if *nothing* is the best thing to do. That was why people ended up with antibiotics for viral infections. That was why they suffered through surgeries when getting some exercise might have done the trick. And, we kids knew, all treatments have side effects and risks—infection, doctor error, allergic reaction. Side effects and risks were no joke. They could leave you with permanent damage, or even dead.

It was a simple question of math. If the risks of not undergoing treatment were greater than the risks of undergoing treatment, then you should have the treatment. But if the risks of treatment outweighed the risks of doing nothing, then you should do nothing. If the treatment was unnecessary in the first place, then the equation was pretty straightforward.

"Scientific method" meant doubting doctors' claims to omnipotence and omniscience just as you doubted ministers' and rabbis' claims. It meant being as skeptical of scientific dogma as you were about religious dogma. It meant not accepting authority for authority's sake but demanding to see the evidence, thinking for yourself, asking questions.

"Does it hurt when you straighten out your thumb?" my father asked.

I straightened out my thumb. "No."

"Does it hurt when you fold it into your palm?" he asked.

"No."

"Does it hurt when you push it all the way back with your other hand?"

I laughed conspiratorially. I knew what was coming. Not being able to push my thumb all the way back with my other hand wasn't exactly a handicap, but *some* people would be convinced it was a sign of a big problem and would demand treatment.

I pushed my thumb back.

"Yes! That hurts!"

"Well," my father said, pursing his mouth in mock seriousness. "Then my recommendation is not to push it way back with your other hand."

8

A FEW DAYS AFTER GLENN AND I MET WITH DEIRDRE, I called Barb.

Barb was all about common sense. Take advantage of modern medicine when it has the best solution; go with lower-tech alternatives when they work just as well or even better. It's why we got along so well. It's why I wanted to talk to her about a home birth.

I phoned her.

"Barb, I'm thinking about doing a home birth."

I expected medical advice. Something that would help me figure out how the "low-tech if possible, high-tech if necessary" philosophy applied in this situation. That's not what I got.

Barb's voice, always so calm and easy, became alarmed. "Lisa, don't do it! If something should happen, you'll have so much to deal with, you won't want to have to ask yourself if you made a terrible mistake! And think about your age!"

I sunk into my seat, stunned. My head jerked up to the window. The lawn, which is usually yellow and patchy by August thanks to heat and sun and drought, was lush from the same heavy rainfalls that had caused terrible flooding across the eastern half of the state earlier that summer. My vegetable garden, however, was in shambles. I had hired someone to look after it for the three weeks Glenn and I had spent in Europe only to come home to knee-high tomatoes lost in shoulder-high weeds. It had been so wet, my would-be gardener had explained, that it had been impossible to do any work. Behind the garden, next to the old goose shed that eight-year-old Adam had rechristened the Dinosaur Clubhouse, lay the ruins of an apple tree and a hackberry tree that had blown down in a windstorm just before the flood. The hackberry had nicked the garage roof, but the contractors and tree people were so overwhelmed with flood-related jobs that they had not yet cleared away the trees or fixed the roof, which was a low-priority job because at least it was not leaking. Hundreds of people in Iowa City—thousands in Cedar Rapids—had been left homeless by the flood, major business districts were still shuttered, and long swaths of the campus lay in ruins. The bickering among property owners, the city, the state, the university, and FEMA was just beginning.

The water had receded, but the entire town was in a state of jittery uncertainty. I felt it every time I looked across the river and saw flood lines eight feet high on the abandoned performing arts auditorium, every time I received an email announcing emergency housing provisions for incoming students. And I felt it as I looked out my window, the emerald-green grass a weirdly snide rejoinder to the tree branches strewn across the back half of my yard. Barb's unexpected outburst completely rattled me.

"Wait, let me explain," I said, anxiously. "I had Adam out-of-hospital, with midwives, and it was really great. I've been seeing the midwives in the hospital, and as far as they're concerned, I'm low risk. From their perspective, my age doesn't make me high risk; it puts me at greater risk for various conditions that would make for a high-risk pregnancy. But they can test for all those things—high blood pressure, gestational diabetes, chromosomal abnormalities, whatever—and if I test negative for all those things, which I do, I'm low risk, my age is irrelevant."

I tripped over my own tongue, afraid that if I stopped talking I might shrink into silence at her disapproval. "But I'm really afraid that once I'm in the delivery room, if the slightest thing happens, the doctors will just look at my age and jump straight to all possible interventions. And I really don't want that."

I still expected to have a discussion about medical matters. Perhaps Barb would remind me of some element of my history that the midwives weren't aware of. Or perhaps she'd mull over my chart and figure it was OK.

"No, Lisa, no." Her voice was urgent. "Listen, maybe I respond too strongly to this for personal reasons. My niece just had a stillbirth. There's nothing more awful. And I can't imagine having to second-guess your decision while you're dealing with something like that."

"But . . . what do you make of the fact that I'm low risk, all that?"

"No, no, no."

We talked a little longer and I hung up, shaking. Not because I was worried about a stillbirth, but because Barb hadn't answered my questions. Who else was I supposed to ask? And I shook because I didn't want Barb to frown on me. Goody-two-shoes.

I TALKED to Glenn that evening. My heart had been pounding ever since the phone call. I'd had to sit down over and over again.

"She really caught me off guard. I've never, ever experienced her like that, and I've known her ten years." We were taking a walk, and the late-summer cicadas were shrieking in the trees.

"So what do you make of it?" Glenn was still not convinced about a home birth either, though he liked the idea that his cousin Isabel, the midwife, was in favor.

"I don't know. It's like you can't have a discussion about the medical issues involved. The whole home birth thing just evokes so much distrust, such a knee-jerk response. And then, on the other side, there's the whole 'medical technology is evil, home birth is peace, love, and lollipops' thing, which just makes me want to smack someone and ask if they really want pre-modern levels of maternal and infant mortality and a life expectancy of forty. I know that's out there, both sides I mean, but I'd really hoped to be able to talk about it with Barb. That's why I like her—she has no ideology about high-tech versus alternative stuff; she just wants to know what the evidence says about one treatment or another. But it just wasn't possible to discuss it with her."

"So now what?"

"I don't know. I mean, I feel like I need to discuss the medical issues before making a decision, but if I can't do it with Barb . . . It's all so polarized."

"But you really respect Barb, right?"

"Well, yes, but I also can't really take our conversation as a discussion about the pros and cons of home birth, aside from whether I'd kick myself afterward if the baby dies. It doesn't help much with the question of whether the baby is more likely to die in a home birth than in a hospital birth, does it? That's what I want to know—are there medical reasons why this would be a bad idea?"

"I want you to do whatever you're comfortable with." Glenn had seen how happy I'd been after we met Deirdre, how tense I'd been every time I contemplated a hospital birth.

I stopped and sighed. "I know you do. I just don't know how to figure out what I'm comfortable with."

"I think you do know what you're *not* comfortable with."

"Yeah, I'm not comfortable with hospital births and obstetricians' enthusiasm for reaching for some machine or some drug because they're in the habit or because they have a timeline for how long labor should last or because they fear a lawsuit. I'm not comfortable with a 15 percent C-section rate on low-risk pregnancies." Glenn winced—he'd forgotten that tidbit. "And I know I had a great experience with Adam's birth."

"Well then?"

"Well then . . . I don't like having a choice of one. I think that's what's really bothering me. I mean, if I were picking an obstetrician, I certainly wouldn't figure that the mere fact that someone had a license means that's the person I want to work with. I'd ask around, probably talk to a few of them, see who I like, see who has a good reputation. But Deirdre's the only game in town. I can't comparison shop."

Glenn nodded. "Heinemans like comparison shopping." My family's frugality is a running joke.

"Yes, Heinemans like comparison shopping. I mean, Deirdre has a great manner, and she talks with a lot of confidence and obviously has a ton of experience, and her references adore her, but how do I know she's the one I'd choose if there were a real choice? In Berlin, there were loads of midwives. We went to the birthing center because it had a good reputation, not just because they happened to be midwives."

We talked and talked. About being caught in Iowa's political battle over midwives. About cousin Isabel's thoughts on the whole business. About exaggerated assumptions about the risk of childbirth and the decrepit state of women over thirty-five. About research showing that planned home birth for low-risk women accompanied by qualified midwives had no higher rates of "bad outcomes" than hospital births for low-risk women. About the fact that people who opposed home birth didn't seem to know the difference between planned and emergency home delivery, between unattended home birth and home birth attended by a trained midwife. About my pregnancy, which was going exactly as it had with Adam: easy, fun, uncomplicated.

We didn't talk about how we would feel if we had a home birth and then the baby died. Who would?

9

BARB COULDN'T HELP ME. AND SO I WAS LEFT WITH the midwives in the hospital.

I had an appointment coming up with Chris, my favorite of the three midwives. But when I arrived, the receptionist told me there had been a scheduling change and so Sara, my least favorite, was taking Chris's shift. I didn't doubt Sara's competence—I'd heard good things from women who had delivered with her. I just didn't feel as comfortable with her personally. Her humor felt a little forced to me, like a mild assault. It made me shrink back.

I would have been nervous anyway. In fact, I was shaking. I didn't want to have this conversation with the very person whose services I might be about to reject. It seemed impolite. And I'd geared up for this conversation with Chris. It was going to be even harder with Sara.

I waited until Sara had finished the exam and confirmed that I was still in great shape.

"I wonder if I can ask something," I ventured.

"Sure, sure, ask away!" Sara said, a little too jovially.

"I am thinking about . . . well, I seem to be having a low-risk pregnancy, and my last delivery went smoothly . . ." No choice but to blurt it out: "I'm thinking about switching over to a home birth."

"Uh huh," Sara nodded vigorously, waiting to hear more.

"But I wanted to see if you think there are reasons I shouldn't do it. Anything in my medical record, anything I might be missing. I mean, I'm obviously older now; I don't know if that changes the equation."

Sara bobbed her head from side to side, and I half expected her voice to come out sing-songy, but it came out Midwestern-flat. "Well, we're hospital people here. We feel more comfortable with a hospital setting. But you're low risk. You're the kind of person who can do a home birth, if that's what you want. Your age doesn't really matter, as long as you're low risk."

Her answer surprised me. I'd expected the hospital midwives to be opposed in principle, and I was glad that Sara seemed to think it would be OK. But yes or no on home birth wasn't the only question I'd come to ask. I'd been prepared to consider home birth even if the hospital midwives disliked the idea, as long as they didn't point to a clear medical indication against it. My other question was: How do I know I've got a good midwife? I wanted help with my choice-of-one problem.

"OK, that's good to know," I said. "But I also wanted to get your reaction to the midwife I'm considering working with. You know, if she has a good reputation. It's a little hard to find that sort of stuff out, and I figure maybe you know some of these people."

"Well, I have to be a little careful about discussing people working out there. It can be a little touchy. But try me." I understood what she was saying, but wished she didn't sound vaguely catty about it.

"Deirdre Bremmer. Do you know her?"

Sara smirked and looked away a moment. "Ohhhhh, her."

She turned back. "All I'll say is this. You gotta think about judgment when you pick a midwife. We had a case here, someone who switched over to her, ended up going over forty-three weeks. Turned out fine, but, you know, *judgment*. You want to think about that."

So what am I supposed to do with that? I thought. The forty-three-week pregnancy had turned out fine. Was it really so obvious that induction, with all the risks it would have carried—more painful labor, likely increasing the need for medication, which can create stress for the baby or make it harder to push, making an emergency C-section necessary—was it really so obvious that induction would have been preferable to letting the pregnancy continue, resulting in a perfectly fine delivery? Had the battle over midwifery affected the hospital midwives' feelings about Deirdre? Deirdre was outspoken and had managed to beat the system by getting licensed and performing home births legally. She was a controversial figure. *And what are my alternatives?* Was I now supposed to ask Sara for a name of someone she liked better? Was I supposed to ask a hospital employee to recommend someone working illegally? If asking about Deirdre had put her in an awkward position, surely she couldn't get into discussions of midwives working illegally.

It wouldn't even be appropriate for me to ask, I convinced myself. And so I didn't. Instead, I thanked her and went home.

I was uneasy with my inability to push further, and glad to get out of there. On the way home, Glenn and I talked about how admirable it was that Sara had said home birth would be fine for me though she herself was more comfortable in the hospital. We talked about the fact that I was in such great physical shape for forty-six. We talked about the fact that Deirdre had been practicing over twenty years with no bad outcomes. When I asked Glenn two years later about our discussion with Sara, he didn't remember that she'd expressed reservations about Deirdre. But I did. And I wondered what would have happened if I had been willing to consider midwives practicing illegally.

Probably if I'd considered other out-of-hospital midwives, I'd have chosen Deirdre anyway. She had two decades of experience and no bad outcomes, and she had a terrific reputation in the natural childbirth community. Maybe I'd have chosen another midwife who would have made precisely the same judgment call when my pregnancy went over a week postdate, because it was a good judgment call—just the one case in a thousand that goes wrong.

But I didn't even do the research. I stopped my search for a midwife, because Deirdre was the only one with a license, and I was a goody-two-shoes. I believed in scientific method, but I didn't do the research.

10

AND SO WE SWITCHED TO DEIRDRE. MY PREGNANCY continued smoothly. Even in the early stages, I'd had no nausea, no fatigue. I had given up running at about four months but then spent several weeks dashing around Central Europe. Once back in Iowa City, I took up aquacize and continued to bike about town. I scrambled to finish a book that I wanted to send to the publisher before Thor came, and had no problem working long hours. Rosemary's new fiancé, a quiet physics instructor named Mick, took us on a tour of post-flood Cedar Rapids—a more depressing scene even than post-flood Iowa City, because Cedar Rapids was so much poorer to begin with. Glenn and I began a birth preparation class. One young straight couple, one young lesbian couple, and one older couple: we all reveled in Iowa City's world of nontraditional parenting.

And I continued to do tai chi. I'd started tai chi after Julia and I had split up. It did for me what meditation does for a lot of people. Body shifting in space but always intact, complete, calm, mindful. Moving meditation.

Soles of feet firmly planted—not forced onto the surface of the floor, but drawn to the core of the earth. Deeply, but not rigidly, so they could lift and take a step without breaking the bond. Head reaching toward to the heavens—not straining upward, just gently connected, as if by a rubber band with just a little tension in it. Arms moving through the air, but always in conversation with the opposite leg, which exerted a gravitational but relaxed pull.

And the core of tai chi: the dantian. Deep in your pelvis, your body's gravitational center, the source of the energy that flows to your arms, your torso, your head, your legs, but which also pulls the energy back, keeping everything gently but firmly connected.

The dantian is your uterus. The tai chi masters don't mention this. Maybe they don't even know; they're mostly men.

Long before I started showing, Thor and my uterus took over my dantian, their three-way symbiosis guiding my tai chi body. They anchored me confidently as I lifted one leg, then the other, so my thigh was parallel to the floor before my shin slowly kicked forward and returned, with arms extended generously to the sides. Golden rooster stands on one leg.

My tai chi instructor noticed, though I said nothing. Don was nicknamed "Gentle Don" by my sister, who had come to visit a couple of years earlier and tagged along to a tai chi class. When Don speaks, the words come slow, soft, but assured, as if they'd been through a course of tai chi themselves.

"You're moving differently," Don said, when I was about five months pregnant. "Your tai chi has improved so vastly over the last months. It's startling."

"It's the pregnancy," I said. "There's a living critter in my dantian. It's a completely different kind of energy."

I worried about suggesting that men, or women who don't experience pregnancy, can't *really* know what tai chi is all about, because their dantian doesn't live in the same way. But Don is generous. With a smile and a nod he welcomed the baby-womb-dantian collaboration to class, the baby-womb-dantian collaboration that kept me perfectly in balance as I lifted my right leg and twirled, relaxed, 360 degrees before gently replacing my foot on the floor and then raising my right leg to do a slow circle from the knee. Lotus flower. Six months, seven months, eight months pregnant.

Toward the very end of my pregnancy, Thor wanted to do aquacize even more than he wanted to do tai chi, and since the meeting times overlapped, I went to aquacize instead. By this time Thor was so heavy that my uterus was fully occupied with him and could no longer be coaxed to help out as much with my tai chi body. Nor did Thor want to carry my arms and legs and torso any longer. He wanted to be carried, by the water in the pool, which buoyed him up and rocked him to sleep.

11

THE FIRST STEP IN A PELVIC EXAM WITH DEIRDRE was sweeping the cats off the examining table. But usually that wasn't necessary, because usually she didn't bother with the table. Most of her prenatal visits took place on the living room sofa.

I have friends who suffer for days in advance of pelvic exams and for days afterward. The exams bring back sensations of sexual abuse, or just bad sex in bad relationships, when they dutifully spread their legs and let things be inserted into a place they couldn't even see because that's what they were supposed to do. Or exams evoke memories of horrible gynecological visits in the past ("Well, I'm sure someone like you knows where to get an abortion") even if the doctor in the room right now is very nice.

I was a doctor's kid and I believed in preventative medicine. I had tolerated pelvic exams since my teenage years by disconnecting my mind from my sexual organs, an especially helpful trick if a med student was along so two people were peering between my legs. Whatever all those people were staring at, wherever all those instruments were sticking out of, those were just body parts. This made pelvic exams doable. But it involved an alienation from my body that wasn't exactly helpful for my intimate life.

Exams with Deirdre were the antihospital experience. No exam gown that left you shivering and couldn't possibly be held closed, even while you were still waiting for the doctor or nurse to come. No sitting on scratchy paper. No stirrups. No speculum. No one shining a bright light into you, head buried between your legs. Deirdre did her exams by touch, eyes meeting mine throughout. She slipped a gloved, lubricated hand inside, and determined the effacement and dilation of the cervix by feel, always giving me a heads-up: "OK, I'm going to touch you now." Only once, when I was going to be traveling out of town barely three weeks before my due date did she do a conventional exam, involving a table and speculum, just to make sure I wasn't farther along than we thought. Exams with Deirdre were downright cozy.

How do I get from my warm memories of those checkups to my agonized memories of my last checkup, the day before I went into labor, a moment of decision-making that might have been fatal? My postdate exams were cozy too, and of course more frequent. Deirdre checked my blood pressure, my cervix, the amount of amniotic fluid. I lay down on the white sofa, filtered light coming through the window, Glenn cross-legged on the floor with the kitten, as Deirdre strapped a heart-monitor belt on my belly and gave me a clicker so I could record Thor's movements. The nonstress tests showed that Thor had a healthy heartbeat and that it increased when I felt movement, just as it should.

And Deirdre talked about what it meant to be postdate. Adam had come five days late, so we shouldn't be surprised if Thor was a bit late, too—some women gestate longer than others. Forty weeks was an average, not a precise schedule. If I were preparing for a hospital delivery, she said, the doctors would probably want an ultrasound around now—I'd just passed a week postdate. At our next visit, on Wednesday, we would talk about whether I should get one. But it probably wouldn't show anything we didn't already know. The key was to make sure Thor was doing ok, which the nonstress tests confirmed. And not to rush things. My cervix was dilated only two centimeters. But it was 80 percent effaced. In other words, things were moving along, and it was unlikely that I'd be waiting much longer.

What if I did have to wait? Deirdre told me of a woman she'd delivered at forty-three-and-a-half weeks. The baby had definitely been ripe, but all was fine. Deirdre's mantra was: baby will come when baby is ready. Just keep close tabs on how things are going. Forty-three and a half weeks sounded long to me, but it didn't matter, because I wasn't going to go that far anyway. My cervix, after all, was 80 percent effaced.

On our walk home, Glenn and I kicked up the fallen leaves, relaxed. To our left and right were sagging but cheerful Halloween pumpkins that were as postdate as I was. Obama-Biden signs celebrated the election that was now nearly a week past. No one was in a hurry to take them down.

Later, all attention focused on the decision to let the pregnancy continue rather than to refer me for an ultrasound once I was a week post-date. The investigator from the Iowa Board of Nursing who questioned me about Deirdre was herself a nurse and looked the part: practical pants and jacket, unstyled shoulder-length blond hair, rimless glasses that were a little too big for her face. Only her supremely unsensible shoes, stiletto heeled and pointy toed, suggested relief at the fact that she now had a job that didn't require her to be on her feet all day.

She had a thick manila folder with my name on it, and flipped through it occasionally to remind herself of a detail she wanted to ask me about. Our interview lasted two hours, and she took detailed notes on a yellow legal pad regarding every aspect of Deirdre's care for me. But she lingered extra long on the tests and advice Deirdre had given me once I was postdate.

"Did you have ultrasounds during the pregnancy?"

"Yes," I said, and described the circumstances of each.

"And after your due date?"

"No."

"Did the subject of an ultrasound come up?"

"Yes, at my last visit Deirdre said we'd talk about it at my next visit."

The investigator looked at me, eyebrows up. "You'd talk about it?"

"Yes."

"She didn't schedule you for one?"

"That's right—we were going to talk about it at the next visit."

What might an ultrasound have found? Placental abruptions are sometimes, but not always, visible on ultrasounds. But the nonstress test indicated that Thor was getting plenty of oxygen, and placental abruptions result in reduced oxygen to the fetus. In other words, the placental abruption almost certainly hadn't happened yet. The autopsy report said that *if* there had been a placental abruption—the report was inconclusive on this point—then it was "of recent onset."

"Does 'recent onset' mean 'during labor'?" I asked the doctor at the reproductive endocrinology clinic two months after the stillbirth. He was a pale man with thin lips and a tight voice who avoided eye contact. "Or does 'recent onset' mean 'within the last few days'?" That is, I thought but didn't ask, might an ultrasound have picked it up?

"We don't even know for sure that there was a placental abruption," he shrugged, uninterested in the questions of a woman so unwise as to have chosen home birth. "Can't tell from this report. We'd have induced seven days postdate."

12

A WEEK AND TWO DAYS POSTDATE, THOR AND I WERE doing fine. My main trouble was round ligament pain. I'd developed it about four weeks before my due date. I'd had it during my first pregnancy, too, toward the end, when I was very big. While walking, the band anchoring the lower part of my uterus to my hip would clench, and I'd instinctively pull up my right leg to avoid sharp pain. Perhaps in the middle of a busy Berlin street. Even in those pre-tai chi days I had great balance, perching on one leg with no warning at all, holding Julia's arm if she happened to be there, but if not, just standing there like a plastic pink flamingo with my good leg plugged firmly into the ground.

A few weeks before I was due the second time around, the flamingo was back. I told Deirdre about it. She recommended I see a chiropractor.

I'd tried chiropractors a couple of times for low-back spasms. The first one tried to cure me by balancing sugar cubes and magnets on my stomach, and I decided I didn't need to go back. My second chiropractor wasn't quite as crazy, but I wasn't sure his little device—something called the "activator"—was really doing much for me. I asked Deirdre if she could recommend anyone. She could: Dr. Dan.

Dr. Dan's practice was in the office space on the second floor of the ritzy new hotel that had gone up a couple of years earlier in downtown Iowa City. Dr. Dan knew what he was doing. Sometimes his adjustments didn't quite do the trick, but most of the time they did. Before a visit, if the ligament was acting up, I was sometimes reduced to a near shuffle when I wasn't balancing on one foot. Afterward I walked like a normal person. Dr. Dan asked my permission to discuss my case at a chiropractors' conference, since it had been a tough nut to crack.

Dr. Dan's greatest triumph was the day before I went into labor. I was already over a week postdate. Coming out of that appointment, I was so loose I could practically skip and dance down the street. I hadn't felt so free in weeks.

The next day, when Glenn and I went to the mall, I felt great, which is saying a lot, because even in the best of circumstances I hate the mall. I walked from one end of the complex to the other to find a new watch for me. When we were done, Glenn wanted to go back to the other end of the mall again because he remembered he needed some jeans. No problem.

That evening, I sprinted through aquacize, my body fast, strong, and flexible. Through the floor-to-ceiling windows at the south end of the pool, we could see the dark night, and across the street we saw the gas station whose fluctuating prices were always a topic of conversation among the swimming ladies. Headlights cruised lazily along the street, and pedestrians walked bundled in their coats, dressed for early winter: protective but not huddled against the cold. Inside, we finished with water angels, floating on our backs and moving our legs and arms up and down, as if we were making snow angels. I let the water hold me and closed my eyes, enjoying the last moments of slow weightlessness that always ended our sessions.

Sometimes leaving the water and moving to land's gravitational pull made me stiff, and hauling my belly home was hard work. Not that day. I walked home in the misty night, under a light freezing rain. Glenn had phoned to say he was going to make salad. Chicken and feta and pears and pine nuts and greens. The air was cool, and I walked tall, straight, with Thor inside me and my legs swinging free. In a couple of hours, the freezing rain would turn to snow. In a couple of hours, I would be in labor.

13

WHEN I THINK OF OUR LAST INNOCENT DAYS, OUR Belle Époque, I think of the pictures we took on Halloween, 2008. The three that ended up in our 2009 calendar. The one I used as my facebook thumbnail for a while: just my torso, in a black knit turtleneck, with a vivid green praying mantis, about six inches long, on my big belly.

I'd decided we needed a photo shoot. It was just a little chilly, but not so much that you needed a coat, or even a jacket—and that was because the sun shone so brightly. It's all in the photos: the dazzling sun, the piercingly blue sky, the puffy white clouds, the long-sleeved-shirt-clad couple as happy as they'd ever be.

We started with a couple of pictures of me in my Halloween costume. Ever since I'd learned my due date—October 30—I'd schemed about being a pumpkin if I was still pregnant on the thirty-first. I wore the big orange turtleneck I'd worn during my pregnancy with Adam, seventeen years earlier. It had turned into comfort clothing, stained and sloppy, to wear around the house in winter. But now it was the perfect pumpkin costume, completed by black leggings and, for the stem, a green knit ski cap. When Adam saw the pictures, he said I looked pretty dorky. He was right. If I'd been more ambitious I would have taped on fabric cut-outs for a jack-o-lantern's eyes, nose, and mouth. But I didn't want to sweat it.

Then the real photo shoot began. I changed clothes—black turtleneck and jeans, about as elegant as I could get at that point—and Glenn wore a beautiful rust-colored, button-down shirt tucked into jeans. I always thought he looked fantastic in that combination, dark shirt showing off his long torso, jeans low on his hips.

My favorites were the pictures on the front porch. We no longer had the perfect Iowa ensemble: the white picket fence, the apple tree, and the front porch swing. The apple tree had blown down in a windstorm, and decades-long rot in the fence posts had required that I tear down the white picket fence. But we still had the front porch swing.

I propped the camera up on the glass-topped table that stood on the porch, set the timer, and we clowned around on the swing. Click-click-click-click-click, ten pictures in quick succession of us flirting with each other, clasping hands, kissing. We looked at them through Adam's animator eyes and realized they would make a good flipbook. I took one that I love of Glenn alone on the swing, laughing so hard his eyes are nearly closed, bent over a little to the side.

We wandered around the side of the house and continued taking pictures. I shot one: Glenn scuffling through the fallen leaves under the chestnut tree, trying to find a chestnut that had hung on the branch the day before. It was one of only two that had matured on the young tree, which had replaced another blown-down apple tree just a few years earlier. I'd had my eye on that chestnut: I wanted to save it, as I always want to save chestnuts. Chestnuts evoke long-past German autumns for me: kicking a soccer ball with Julia's brother's son, my nephew; inhaling the throat-burning smoke of the first soft-coal fires of the season, before Berlin banned coal ovens; laughing as my niece demonstratively tossed off her cap while climbing in the playground.

Glenn shot one: Lisa by the Obama-Biden sign, where the bright light made me squint. Adam's first political memory was of the 2000 election, and he had known nothing of American politics other than the Bush presidency. Now we were days away from emerging from the darkness. We were going to have an Obama baby! Yes, Obama was sure to disappoint, but for the first time I understood parents who named their children after public figures: Franklin Delano Roosevelt, or Mother Theresa.

We went to the driveway, propped the camera on the tent-trailer and put on the timer again, to get photos of us in front of the Adammobile. Click-click-click-click-click.

And then to the garden bed. Glenn took pictures as I walked, as I bent over and buried my hand in the weeds— and thanks to the flooding that summer there was nothing but weeds. But no, there *was* something other than weeds: a huge, angular, bright green praying mantis. When was the last time I'd seen such a thing?

Adam was the one who found bugs. When he'd been smaller, he'd adored them. *He* was the one who discovered huge cicadas and tiny inchworms. *He* was the one who could sneak up silently, reach out a hand, and in a flash capture an unsuspecting cricket. *He* was the one who picked up bugs and let them crawl all over his body and then, once evening fell, drew pictures of them.

But Adam wasn't here, and this praying mantis needed to

be picked up. Gently, gently, I eased it into my hand, and onto the left side of my belly, vertical, head facing mine as I straightened up. Glenn took pictures—far enough to see me laughing as the praying mantis approached my neck, and so close my face wasn't visible, only the insect's still, vibrant green against the black of my shirt.

During the lull between Christmas and New Year's in 2008, six weeks after Thor's birth and death, I made our calendar for 2009. Our calendar-making tradition had begun when Julia's mother had put together photos from 1991, the year I was pregnant with Adam, into a calendar for 1992. After that Julia and I took over, and soon the calendars included both photos of Adam and his artwork from the previous year. Once he was a teenager, Adam objected to calendars featuring only him: he said it was embarrassing. And so we included pictures of everyone in the family.

Three prints from that Halloween photo session made the cut. In another picture I held a big morel mushroom I'd picked during a late spring visit to a friend's farm in Wisconsin; I was pregnant but not yet showing. One picture showed Adam dressed as a mime for his school's annual film fest, which students traditionally attended in wild costumes (Adam mimed his acceptance speeches for his two awards). In another, Glenn and Adam laughed in a café in Chicago as we took a break from the youth film fest where one of Adam's films was screened. That picture sometimes made tears come to my eyes: it had been awkward when Glenn had come into fifteen-year-old Adam's life, but by the time we visited Chicago a little over a year later, they were relaxed and easy with each other.

But really, 2008 was the year of Thor. His conception,

gestation, birth, and death—his entire abbreviated life—had passed in 2008. We had dozens of photos of Thor from the hospital, from our visits to the funeral home, and from his visits home. But we didn't want to put them in the calendar, which would hang in the breakfast nook. Adam's friends often sat there, and it would be uncomfortable for them to look up from their milkshakes to a picture of a dead baby. Adam himself didn't want to see photos of Thor.

And so Thor was represented in the calendar by one picture only, on the cover, so it didn't hang exposed with any month. The picture showed Thor's leg band from the hospital, laid flat on a table. It consisted of four lines.

On the first were the words: "Eighty-eight, patient."

The second read, sphinx-like: "DOB: 01/01/1850 ? age M."

The third line had a barcode.

And the fourth line included an ID number: 03-89188-4, and a date and time stamp: 11/12/08 02:17.

III

Verdun

GLENN AND I ARE IN OUR HOSPITAL ROOM. IT IS DARK outside, and the blinds are shut tight. Opposite the bed is a dark wooden cabinet that houses a TV and above the TV cabinet is a clock, and just as we know that the TV doesn't matter because it's off and will stay off, we know that the clock matters a great deal. The clock on the wall ticks loudly and reminds us that time is short.

It's 5:20 on the morning of November 12, 2008. Glenn is holding Thor, biting his lip as he looks down at him. This is the only 5:20 we'll ever have with our baby.

I sit propped up by pillows in my hospital bed, the same bed where the blue hordes palpated my belly, the same bed where I argued with the medical examiner. To the right and behind me is the counter where the nurses stack their papers and prepare their medications, but no one stands there now. The nurses have gone. They have gone because we have Thor, and they know we won't have him for long. They will let my next blood draw, my next blood pressure check, wait until after he is gone.

Only three people remain in the room, and of the three only two are alive. But we must will ourselves to imagine that Thor is still with us, that he has a glimmer of life not yet completely extinguished. He must be one of three people present for this scene, not an inert prop.

We try hard to imagine. We suspend disbelief. This will be our entire lifetime with our child.

WHEN THEY bring Thor to me, I feel all the tension of the last hours slip out of the room like a sigh. Finally, we've arrived at our destination.

This is our destination: I can hold Thor in my arms. This is what I've been waiting for for nine months. This is what's been imminent since I went into labor a few hours earlier. This moment was delayed, because all sorts of other things have gotten in the way: the EMT people taking Thor downstairs to the kitchen, the ambulance ride, the light blue hordes palpating my belly, Glenn going to see Thor separately, my having to argue with the man from the medical examiner's office. But finally, finally, the moment has arrived: I can have Thor.

There is something terribly elemental about that moment, about looking forward to it in the few minutes between my conversation with the boss from the medical examiner's office and the time they bring Thor. Something so elemental that even death doesn't get in the way. Thor was inside me, and now he is rightfully outside. He is outside but he belongs in my arms, cradled naked against my breast, just a ribcage away from where he's been curled up all those months.

Once upon a time, stillborn babies were whisked away and the parents didn't even see them. But now hospitals have changed their practice, and parents can have and hold their stillborn babies, to say goodbye.

No one seems to have thought of the fact that first the parents have to say hello. Perhaps that's why they think half an hour is enough. But we have six hours.

Thor will not change during those six hours. He will not be freshly born when I get him, then six hours old when I give him back. He will not be awake, then asleep. He will not first be unwashed, then washed; first hungry, then sated; first crying, then content, then crying again. He will be exactly the same at the end of the six hours as he was at the beginning. Just a little cooler, a little stiffer, but we aren't thinking about that. And so the six hours will be a moment, not an expanse of time. But it will be a moment that will stretch out, like silly putty that resists snapping as you stretch it farther and farther, and even though you know it won't stretch forever, for the moment what's amazing is that it stretches as far as it does.

This is what I want to do in those six hours. To take that moment, in which Thor will not grow six hours older, and inhabit it fully. To fully absorb Thor, because this will be our only chance.

And because this is so important, other things can wait. Like crying. Like thinking about Thor's absence. I will have a lifetime to explore Thor's absence, every inch of it; to acquaint all my senses with it, to inhabit it. Any time we spend crying now, bewailing his death, will be time lost to things like singing to him, touching him, things we have only a few hours to do. Thor's absence will not last just a moment, not even a stretched-out moment. It will occupy time. First he will be dead a day, then a week, then a month, then a year. I will have the rest of my life to explore it, and its exploration will require the rest of my life. But the time to explore Thor's absence is not now. Now is the time to absorb Thor's presence.

I have no script for this time, no instructions. But I know what to do.

I touch him.

I touch his face, his narrow cheeks, his hard brow. I use the tip of my index finger. I cradle the back of his head and move my hand down to feel the curve of his skull. I trace the hump of his chin, starting from the tape that holds the intubation tube in his mouth. I continue down his long throat to his collarbone.

As I support him with my left arm, I use my right hand to pull the blanket away from his chest. I fill my hands with him. I spread out my fingers, making my hands as big as I can. One on his back, the other across his chest and stomach. My hands do not meet, because this is a big baby.

I try another hold: one hand on each side of Thor's head, fingers overlapping at the back. Now I have a feel for his head, and his torso. My hands rest. They will want to remember these proportions.

I unfold the rest of the blanket. I see the stump of the umbilical cord, brown, with a piece of gauze held in place with a clamp. I see the small, uncircumcised penis, the wrinkled, dark scrotum. I see how fat his thighs are, and turn him around to see if the buttocks from which they extend are equally fat. The lower legs look slim in comparison. Pegs protrude from the shins, the pegs that were to deliver drugs directly to the bone because the veins were too small; I must be careful of those pegs. His feet are wrinkled and crusty with yellowish meconium.

I hold Thor under his arms so his feet rest on my lap, as if he were standing. I support his head.

I see that Thor's eyes are half open. He looks like he's look-ing at me. I meet his gaze. I tell him with my eyes how much I love him. I lean my brow against his brow, my nose against his nose. I close my eyes.

I breathe in. I smell his smell. It is earthy, bloody, unwashed. I lift him higher, until my nose is buried in his neck. I smell him again, inhaling deeply.

I sit Thor on my lap. I tell him that he is my beautiful, beautiful baby. I tell him that I love him, and that I will always love him. I caress his cheek and tell him the same thing. I kiss his face and say it again.

I invite Glenn over with my eyes. I hold Thor up so Glenn can take him. I watch how Glenn cradles Thor as he stands, how he looks down at him, thick eyebrows arched.

We talk about Thor. About how big he is. About how his eyes are open. We let conversation falter.

I follow Glenn with my eyes as he sits down by my bed. We hold Thor together. I put my face to Thor's as Glenn does the same from the other side.

We close our eyes. We breathe deeply.

I pull back as Glenn takes Thor's hand. He slips his finger into the hollow between Thor's curled fingers and the palm of his hand. I look at the wrinkles on the back of Thor's tiny fin-gers with their fingernails already gone purple, the solidity and straightness of Glenn's big finger.

I take Thor back. I sing him a song that I make up as I go along, a song with few notes and few words, but which goes on a long time. I rock Thor as I sing to him.

I look into Thor's eyes. I realize, suddenly, what his eyes are saying to me. He is asking why he has died. He is saying he had looked forward to meeting me. He knew my warmth and my voice from inside. He wanted to feel my arms and my lips once he was outside. He wanted to see me. He thought that coming out would be the beginning, not the end.

I am his mother. He doesn't know who else to ask.

His mouth is covered with tape.

THIS IS what stays with me about those hours with Thor. His heft burned into the muscles of my arms, matching the heft that had just been in my belly. The softness of his cheek against my rough fingers. His smell thick in my nostrils, following the flow of cool air as it bends to travel downward, high at the back of my throat. The solidity of his back against my splayed hands, the fine hairs on the top of his head under my thumbs, the half-closed eyes. His eyes boring into mine the thoughts that his voice could not utter, not even in a scream or a whimper. It was a magical time, because I had Thor and was not yet grieving for him. Because I was in his presence, not his absence.

But when I stop to think about that morning, I know that we were not alone the whole time. Deirdre and Jeannie came in early on, and in my mind's eye I see them on the sofa, sitting uncomfortably forward, hands folded on their knees. They look very far away, though the sofa is just a few feet from the bed, under the window with the blinds pulled tight.

I am propped up in my hospital bed. Thor lies curled in my left arm. My right hand rests lightly on the back of his head. He is mine, mine.

I ask Deirdre what happened.

"A sudden placental abruption, I'm pretty sure," is what

she says. "Your placenta separated from the uterine wall. That would explain the bleeding. What happens then is that the baby no longer gets oxygen, its adrenaline shoots up because it senses danger, it empties its bowels, and then it tries to breathe, because its lungs are mature and know to try to get oxygen. But instead they get feces-filled meconium. He suffocated."

I do not remember Jeannie saying anything. I do not remember any other part of that conversation, but I assume Deirdre must have asked if we wanted them to stay around, and we said no, and so they left. I do remember that Deirdre stopped at my bed, bent over, kissed my forehead, and slipped away.

I remember that someone from the medical examiner's office came in and asked me to tell him the sequence of events of the evening. I told him, calmly, with Thor lying on my chest. My memory of the birth was clear. He asked if Glenn had anything to add. I don't remember what Glenn said.

Someone else, maybe a nurse or a social worker, asked if we wanted a chaplain and if so, which chaplain? Glenn and I stared dumbly at each other. We were atheists. But echoes of ritual from our childhoods still sounded in our heads. I said, "Let's have them come. I don't want to not do it, then regret that we didn't have this one little bit of ritual." We asked for the Protestant chaplain and the rabbi.

When the rabbi arrived, slight, with his well-trimmed white beard, a flicker of recognition crossed his face. He knew me from around town, knew that I was in some way Jewish, knew that I had nothing to do with the Jewish community. I felt guilty at having dragged him to the hospital at six in the morning for such a bad Jew, one whose dead baby lay naked on his back on a blanket on his mother's lap, limbs sprawled over her legs, testes dark and prominent. After the Methodist pastor recited her blessing, the rabbi murmured his service in rapid-fire Hebrew, saying "speak with me" at the handful of iterations of the Sh'ma. I mumbled along, by now no longer in the bed but seated in a reclining chair. Glenn asked the nurse to take a picture of us when it was over, and when I look at the picture now, I see the rabbi and pastor struggling between smiling reflexively for the camera and their habit of wearing somber expressions in the presence of death. I imagine they wondered what exactly we were after.

A social worker who specialized in organ and tissue donation came in to ask if we wanted to donate Thor's heart valves. With infants, she told us, that was the only possible donation—everything else was too small. Yes, we told her, we wanted to donate Thor's heart valves. I held Thor in my arms, felt his skin against mine.

There was some question about eligibility for donation since I traveled frequently to Europe so perhaps his heart valves would transmit Mad Cow Disease. The social worker came back later in the morning to tell us that the heart valves would be accepted. Months later we learned that they had gone to a baby in North Carolina. We didn't learn any details about the baby who got them, though I wished we had.

I do not remember what the social worker looked like, even though Glenn and I liked her. She seemed like a grown-up.

I do remember what Beth, the night nurse, looked like. She was young and short and had very smooth skin. She had dark curly hair down to her chin.

When Beth's shift was over she buried her face in my shoulder and cried. It was her first death. Labor and delivery nurses don't expect to have to deal with death. Labor and delivery is supposed to be the happy ward. If you work in oncology, *then* you steel yourself to deal with death.

I patted Beth's back and comforted her. I was old enough to be her mother.

Was Thor on my lap during this time? In Glenn's arms? I don't remember.

Thor in my arms, his weight against my chest, his cheek against mine, as I nod and listen to the social worker tell me that only heart valves can be donated, the heart valves that at that moment are at about the level of my shoulder.

Thor seated upright in my lap, leaning against my belly, my arms crossed across his chest, my hands grasping his wrists, playing a sort of patty-cake as I recount for the man from the medical examiner's office the last evidence of Thor's having been alive: the heartbeat Deirdre had heard on her first visit.

My arms and chest and heart and gut, everything from the collarbone down, enveloping Thor. My brain and ears and mouth, everything from the chin up, talking with the nurse, the social worker, the medical examiner, whatever adult wanted something from me. My throat struggling in between, to voice the words I needed to say to the staff, to sing and murmur to Thor. My throat tightening and choking from the conflict.

THE CONFLICT ended when Adam arrived.

Adam didn't want to see Thor. And so when he and Julia arrived, we had a nurse lay Thor down in the next room.

Hugs all around, murmurings of sympathy. Julia and Adam sat, emissaries from the outside world, the real world, the world beyond social workers and nurses and medical examiners and dead babies.

Conversation faltered before it started.

"How are you doing with all this?" I asked Adam.

He shrugged. "It doesn't really mean much to me." He stopped, afraid he'd said the wrong thing. "I mean, I'm really sorry for you guys. But it just doesn't affect me that much."

There is a kind of lucidity that comes with being at the center of disaster. The part of you that gets distracted by the white noise of daily life finally shuts up, and what's left of your mind sees with absolute clarity and simplicity.

The fog of the last hours vanished in an instant, the alternative universe of MommyDaddyDeadBaby displaced by the real world of sixteen-year-old Adam, who the night before had had wings for dinner and who in a couple of hours would be in a school full of kids counting down the days till Thanksgiving break. I saw what Adam faced over the next weeks. People would expect him to be terribly sad, and he just wasn't. He would either have to pretend—and he'd just shown he wouldn't—or he would have to deal with people who thought that if he wasn't brokenhearted, then he must be cold-blooded.

But Thor hadn't been part of Adam's life. Thor had been a cool and exciting thing that was going to happen in the future, but some cool and exciting things that are going to happen in the future don't pan out in the end, and then—if your life is good anyway—you don't obsess about what might have been; you just keep going with what's already good. Adam was sixteen, gearing up to finish high school, working on his art, hanging out with his friends. There was a lot that was good.

"That's OK," I said, looking closely at him. "You should have your own experience of this, whatever that is. It's not going to be the same as ours. Don't worry about what other people think you should be feeling."

Just because you're lucid doesn't mean you don't come off sounding like a self-help manual.

After Adam and Julia left, the nurses brought Thor back to our room. I held him and rocked him and sang to him some more, but it wasn't quite the same. The night shift was over. The staff that had experienced our arrival, my emergency treatment, the announcement of Thor's death, our first hours with him, had gone home. The morning staff was concerned with my blood pressure and iron levels, not with our loss, which they hadn't shared.

Thor's eyes were now almost completely shut, perhaps because he'd been lying on his back for an hour in the next room while Julia and Adam visited. I wondered if his eyes would suddenly fly open when I held him upright, like a doll's, but they didn't. Thor, who a few hours earlier had seemed alive enough to ask me why this was the end, not the beginning, had slipped away. I hadn't been able to answer his question, and he had no more use for me.

At ten o'clock a social worker stepped into the room. The daylight, bright by now and unimpeded by the blinds, which someone had flicked open some time earlier, chided us with its presence and the social worker's.

"*It's morning now,*" the light said. "*People are at work now, at school. Outside, traffic lights are cycling red-green-yellow. Retirees are taking their dogs out for a walk. That business with Thor, it's all over. That was last night. You know what daytime means.*"

Glenn looked up from the sofa at the social worker. "It's time?"

"Yes, it's time."

I lifted Thor from my lap, held him upright, and looked at his face. His eyes were closed. He looked like he had already left. Like a baby who had insisted on being carried, but had then fallen asleep in your arms, soundly, so now he wouldn't object if you lay him down in his crib, switched off the lights, and left the room.

I drew Thor to me and kissed his forehead. I looked hard at him, to remember at least this closed, absent face, since the other one was already gone. I was tired.

"Bye, Thor," I said. "You have to go now."

I handed Thor to Glenn, who was already standing. Glenn took Thor in his arms, kissed him, turned around, walked the few steps to the social worker, and handed him over. The social worker left with Thor, and Glenn turned to face me, he at one end of the room, I at the other, our eyes meeting over the yawning emptiness between us.

2

AT AROUND FOUR THAT AFTERNOON, THE STAFF
started discharge procedures. There wasn't much left to do or
say. I was given a packet of instructions: how to stop lactation
when my milk came in, how to ease any pain in my stretched
and swollen vagina, how much bleeding was too much. I signed
some papers. Glenn and I collected our things and stuffed them
into the tote bags he'd brought with us to the hospital: my
robe, my slippers, our cell phones—those had come with us—
and some new items: the packet from Touching Hearts, the
hospital's program for parents of miscarried or stillborn babies
(web addresses for support groups, the phone number for Iowa
City Hospice); a plastic ziplock bag with a clip of Thor's hair,
so fine and short the hospital staff had had trouble getting their
fingers around a clump substantial enough to cut; two CDs
of photos taken with the camera the nurses kept at the station; my armband and Thor's leg band; papers from the Organ
Donor's Network; a little blue cap, crocheted by a volunteer
from Touching Hearts. We left the Touching Hearts blanket
behind—we figured someone else could use it, and the cap was
enough of a souvenir.

I went to the bathroom one last time—by this time I
could easily manage on my own—and we put on our coats
and headed out. Past the nurses' station, where only one or

two nurses sat, past the glass-walled back room where they lounged when they took a break, past the multistoried, glass-walled atrium, which had been stripped of its decorations and was dark because it was in the process of transformation into new office space. An elevator took us to the exit where Julia would pick us up. I didn't recognize it and still can't place it in the hospital's geography—neither the interior, nor the external approach for cars—though I've been in that hospital a hundred times before and since. There was a bench facing the driveway: from there you could watch for the car that's coming to pick you up. But someone else, a slightly older woman, was sitting on one side of the bench, and I didn't want to sit next to anyone. Glenn offered to pull up a chair, with a soft, blue cushion, to a perpendicular spot, across from the big sliding doors, so I could still see the cars approaching. But I felt no need to watch. I went to the long bench opposite the one that was occupied, blond wooden legs and the same blue-fabric cushion as the chair, with its back to the approach. I told Glenn he could go closer to the door and watch for Julia.

Darkness was falling, though it wasn't really dark yet. Twenty-four hours earlier I'd been on my way to aquacize; night had fallen while I was there. Now I watched the cars as they pulled out, slowly, the red brake lights relaxing as they moved farther away. The woman across from me, dark haired and a little plump, sat dully, eyes fixed on the window. Glenn stood in his red jacket near the chair he'd offered me. The three of us were as far apart from each other as we possibly could be, given the space available, like the points of a triangle drawn by a very efficient architect trying to maximize interior space.

Glenn nodded when he saw Julia's car and came to pick up

the bags, which were slumped next to me on the bench. I rose, and we walked out, the automatic doors sliding smoothly, with a low whirr, before us. The woman on the bench sat as dully as ever. Julia apologized for having taken so long: it was just after five, and she'd had to make her way through what passed for rush hour traffic in Iowa City. I told Glenn to take the front seat; I'd sit in the back.

Julia's car was tidy, like her house, like her office. The sound of the doors closing was firm, low, adult—not like the chaotic, undisciplined clank of the doors on my car, ten years older than Julia's. Julia pulled out, and I looked over my shoulder, through tears, at the maze of boxy buildings that made up the hospital complex.

I'd wanted to leave—no sense spending another night in the hospital when there was no medical need. I'd rather be at home. But as we pulled away and I looked at the neat row of square windows, each one lit with an identical intensity, casting the walls of the buildings into greater darkness, I thought: somewhere in that building is Thor. Somewhere. I didn't know where. Which window, which row of windows? Probably the morgue and the autopsy rooms are in the basement, I thought; dead patients don't care about natural light. Thor was in that building, and I was driving away. Against the murmur of Julia and Glenn talking in the front seat, I craned my head over my shoulder and leaned toward the back window, trying to stay just a little closer, reaching my hand up against the window. Goodbye, Thor.

3

PEOPLE OFTEN SPEAK OF THE DAYS FOLLOWING A terrible event as a blur. The period after Thor's death was many things for me. It was brilliant; it was dark. It was impenetrable; it was translucent. It was like the finest of particles; it was like a thick syrup. The one thing it was *not*, was a blur. I have never experienced the world around me, never experienced my inner world, more sharply than I did in those days. My senses were heightened, with scents more pungent, colors more crystalline, sounds more textured, than ever before or since. And I was acutely aware of every thought that passed through my head— no, I was acutely aware of every *element* of every thought. It was as though it were not enough to see the fascinating detail of water in a cup, its mysterious quality of being utterly *there* yet completely transparent, to notice every ripple in the surface and the precise way it bent the light. I saw the hydrogen and oxygen atoms and their jiggling tension with each other; I saw each molecule's dance around its neighbors.

I don't know why this was. Is there some psychobiological explanation, having to do with a sharpening of the senses in response to extreme duress? Or was it my realization that my time with Thor was now critically short and I couldn't afford to sleepwalk through even a split second of it? Even if Thor wasn't with me, this still was my time with him. This was the time when he was within reach, just a ten-minute drive away in the funeral home, not below the earth. This was the time when my body still bore his traces, the skin around my belly still loose: adequate, if stretched out, to hold a full-term baby should one find its way back in there. I would not dare to miss seeing the shape of a single tree across the street from our home. I would not dare to miss feeling a single bend of my now unencumbered hips. I would not dare to let the smell of the soap on the kitchen sink get by me, nor how it felt first to take a breath in the warm living room filled with heavy-scented flowers, then to step outside and fill my lungs with the fresh, late-autumn air. The crumble of the meat in the cabbage rolls, the smoothness of the carrot soup. The ridge of Adam's eyebrow, the muscle in Glenn's shoulder. The volume of all my senses was increased a few percent, not so much that light and sound and flavors glared intolerably, just so everything shimmered with a brightness that let nothing escape, that imprinted everything absolutely in my mind's memory, in my body's memory.

THE MORNING after we came home from the hospital, I woke with a start, expecting to feel Thor kick. Instead, I found the loose, wrinkled folds of my collapsed belly. I reached for a piece of paper and a pen and wrote: "11/13/08 6:30 a.m. I wake expecting to feel Thor kick."

Over the next days, weeks, months, a flood of words came out. I grasped my little booklet as I went from home to funeral parlor, park to cemetery, kitchen to living room. Torrents of words. I had never so much as kept a journal before.

And screams came out. Screams and sobs and wails. Pain packaged as sound, as air, as liquid, as solid, as words, as flailing movement. Pain packaged as tears and sweat and blood and urine and feces and hair. Pain trying to get out, looking for ever more inventive means of escape, because it was crowded in there, in me. There was no space for more pain, I would burst. But for every bit that found a way out, ten new little pillows of pain ballooned into being to fill the vacuum, fast-growing tumors frantically seeking their own exit.

The pain settled at night, and I slept. I slept well. But I groaned. Every few seconds, every couple of minutes, another little tuft of pain rose from my gut through my throat and out my mouth, like the exhaust of a car that is idling but has not been shut off.

But now I was awake.

I put down the pen and scrap of paper. I dragged myself out of bed, to the bathroom to change the sanitary napkin that had caught the last few hours of Thor's waste, and crawled back into bed. Glenn lay asleep, the crusted salt trace of a tear drawing a line from the outside corner of his eye to his ear. He stirred as I slipped back into bed.

"What time is it?" he mumbled, barely audible.

"6:30."

He pulled me to him and buried his face in my hair. We had an appointment at the funeral home at 9:30.

4

IOWA CITY IS A TWO-FUNERAL-HOME TOWN. WHEN they'd asked in the hospital which funeral home we wanted—this was the question that had made me cry, after I'd spent hours playing with Thor, and Glenn had wondered at my happiness in being with him—we'd picked Lensing, because everyone we knew who had died had gone there. Glenn thought he'd met Mike Lensing once at a party, years ago. Julia said she'd run into him and his boyfriend on Halloween, while she was walking her dog by his house, which was around the corner from hers.

And so, after a wordless breakfast, we drove to Lensing. This is what you do the day after you have a baby. You go to the funeral home.

It was a blindingly bright day, and the light cut especially harsh because we had spent the previous day indoors, in the hospital room, emerging only at dusk. The streets were silent. We were still the only ones in the world, Glenn and I. But that was about to end. We had an appointment.

From the outside, Lensing looks like a suburban ranch house: a single-story brick structure with an overly generous driveway and columns that don't really belong. Inside, it's dark, with heavy drapes, gas fireplaces, and framed newspaper clippings of old Iowa City hanging on the patterned wallpaper. It looks like it's trying to look Victorian, because maybe that's how funeral homes are supposed to look.

Mike Lensing sat us down at a walnut-stained table and let out a sigh. "I got the report from the hospital," he said. He was a big man, perhaps a few years older than I, with short dark hair parted to the side and rimless glasses. His voice had a soft twang. "I am *so* sorry."

Of course he was sorry, I thought peevishly. He was director of a funeral home. What else would he say?

Glenn murmured a few words of acknowledgment.

"Why don't you tell me what happened."

I shrugged and avoided his gaze. "The baby died," I said. What did he think had happened?

Mike nodded. He wanted more.

I told him the story that was already beginning to feel formulaic: healthy pregnancy, no, ridiculously easy pregnancy, everything fine going into labor, then as far as we could tell a sudden placental abruption, the baby stopped getting oxygen, got an adrenaline rush, emptied his bowels, tried to breathe, and suffocated on the feces-filled amniotic fluid. Meconium aspiration. I shrugged again. Was that enough? I wasn't interested in his canned words of sympathy.

Mike folded his hands, shook his head downward at the table, clicked his tongue against the roof of his mouth, looked up, and said:

"*That's* the shits."

MIKE'S COMPLETE lack of orthodoxy enveloped me like a blanket. He never showed a hint of the practiced seriousness that I'd dreaded, suspecting that's probably what people learn at funeral director school. Instead, he treated Thor as a human being. A *baby* human being, and babies aren't at all serious. Babies are cute. They make you laugh.

"What's his name again?" Mike asked a few minutes later, rifling through some papers.

"Um . . . Thor," I said, rolling my eyes inwardly at what now seemed like an infantile joke. Now I'd have to explain to everyone that our dead baby's name was Thor. "That wasn't supposed to be his name," I said, self-consciously. "It was just kind of his silly fetal name . . ."

But Mike didn't seem to feel any explanation was necessary.

"Right, Thor!" He grinned, and clasped his hands together as if someone had just brought him a big ice cream sundae. "I remember when I first read it, I had to think of that newscaster, oh, what's his name? You know, one syllable, kind of tough, dramatic . . . and then the last name, like lightning or something?"

"Wolf Blitzer?" Glenn asked.

"Yes, him! Thor! Wolf!" Mike shot each name out, as if to test the feeling of his diaphragm pushing the air out of his lungs with each vowel. "Kind of funny-dramatic, very . . . *manly*, but, you know, sort of silly." Mike blinked with delight.

Neither Glenn nor I had ever organized a funeral before. We had never given the slightest thought to what we might want our own funerals to be like. Once the pastor and rabbi had said their blessings in the hospital, we knew, that would be the end of our religious observance. There would be no church or synagogue service, and that meant we had to figure it out for ourselves. How many things had we over-researched, like what speakers to buy or prices for a plane ticket to Berlin on the eighth as opposed to the ninth or the various options in cloth diapers? Now we had to plan a funeral, and we didn't have any idea of where to start.

We tossed out ideas as Mike listened. Should we bury Thor this weekend? My sister and Glenn's had already booked flights to come into town just a week later, for Thanksgiving, to meet each other and the new baby. Maybe we should postpone till then so it would be easier for our families to fly in. But then lots of our friends would be out of town. We could bury him now but have the service later. No, I didn't like that.

What is the perfect time to bury Thor? I thought, the space above my eyes curdling in on itself as I listened to our words. *The perfect time is no time. We can't bury him. We just got him.*

The effect of Mike's charm waned temporarily.

What kind of coffin did we want? Mike called it a "casket." More polite, like saying someone "passed" instead of "died" and burying the "remains" instead of the "body." Mike had only one infant casket on hand. It looked like a picnic cooler on the inside: lined with gleaming white plastic and just the right dimensions for a large family outing. The outside was white, too, with molding and some kind of design on the lid, I forget what—a little lamb or something. It was waterproof and airtight, made to preserve the "remains," to slow decomposition. The idea was that if you moved, you might want to dig up ("disinter") your baby and rebury it near your new home.

Mike saw my expression. He said he could order us a different casket. Something simple, made of wood.

More questions. Did we want a folding program, or a

bookmark-sized card? Could we use photos of Thor on the program? Was it OK to use photos of a dead body, we wondered, because that was all we had, would that freak people out? How about a bulletin board with photos? Music? Who would lead the service? Who would speak?

That curdling in the space above my eyes again.

Between us, we knew exactly one thing, which is to say that Glenn knew one thing and I knew nothing. Glenn wanted an open-casket service, an opinion he expressed with a conviction that cut a bright purple swath through our fog of indecision. He wanted people to know Thor was a real person, which was different from knowing that my pregnancy was over but there was no baby. There was a baby. The baby was a boy. He was pale, not swarthy. He had fine, light hair, not thick locks. He was big and chunky, not slender and leggy. Glenn wanted Thor to be a presence, not an absence. Open casket.

Which didn't solve the problem of deciding what kind of casket, what kind of service, what kind of programs, music, photos. Which didn't solve the problem of my throat's rebellion against planning Thor's funeral.

Mike stated the obvious. Maybe we weren't ready to put something together in the next couple of days. Maybe we should wait till Thanksgiving week.

And so the one thing we did that morning was to sign Thor up for embalmment to buy ourselves some time. If Glenn and I *had* ever thought about funerals, we surely would have decided we wanted Thor's body left in its natural state, or at least the state it was in after the autopsy and the organ donation. But we hadn't thought about it, and now we needed time, and embalming was required by law if you didn't bury or cremate (leaving "cremains"! like Craisins, or Cranapple!) within three days.

And then, just when I thought we were done and was reaching down to pick up my purse, Mike said it:

"Well, you just come and visit him *any time* you want."

My hand, grasping a soggy tissue, froze in midair. I looked up at him. "We can visit him?"

"Of *course* you can visit! Just give us a call in advance, so we can take him out of the fridge and let him warm up—it's nicer that way. Oooh, what a little sweetie he is, so cute! Now, you'll have to wait a little while, till we get him embalmed. But tomorrow afternoon—that would be just fine."

I gaped at him. I had thought I was saying goodbye to Thor when we'd left the hospital. I was almost as grateful as if Mike had told us he could bring Thor back to life.

Having your dead loved ones nearby used to be normal. But nowadays you're supposed to keep corpses in their proper place, which may be the morgue, may be the funeral home, but most important is somewhere *else*, away from the living. But this isn't the law. It's just that no one bothers to tell grieving families their options. Unless you discover the home funeral movement, which we didn't. Unless Mike is your funeral director, which he was.

"Shoot, you can take him home if you want! Take him over night, spend some time with him. Maybe you have some friends who'd like to visit with him? It'll be fine, just keep him in a room that's cool."

Our bedroom, I thought, my head spinning. *We always turn down the heat there during the day, to save energy. And at night the whole house is cool anyway.*

But of course that wasn't the point. Our bedroom was where Thor was supposed to have slept with us, where I was supposed to have nursed him.

This was when I understood: Thor was our baby. He did not belong to the hospital. He did not belong to the funeral home. He was ours.

We could bring him home.

I DO NOT BELIEVE IN GOD. I DO NOT BELIEVE IN AN afterlife. I have never been one of those people to say, "I'm spiritual but not religious." I'm not even quite sure what that means, but I think I'm neither spiritual nor religious.

But I do believe in the power of the imagination.

When Adam was in preschool, one of his favorite activities was to "tell Winnie the Pooh." By the time he was in first grade, Winnie the Pooh had retired and we would "tell Wolf and his cousins." That meant Adam and Julia and I would spin stories about Winnie the Pooh, or Wolf and his cousins (whom Adam had made up), as we drove or walked or got ready for bed or ate our dinner. The stories went on for weeks, months: each day we'd pick up where we'd left off the day before. Winnie the Pooh and his friends, and Wolf and his cousins, were central characters in Adam's life for years. In Julia's life and in mine as well.

Once I asked Adam if Wolf and his cousins were real. "Oh, no," he said casually, "They're not real. I just like to think about them." Adam didn't know this was supposed to be a loaded question; he didn't know that some parents fretted that their children couldn't distinguish between fantasy and reality. I wasn't one of those parents, and neither was Julia. We didn't worry whether Adam could distinguish between fantasy and reality—not because we were entirely sure that he could, but because we didn't think it really mattered. If he didn't know the difference now, then it was nice for him to live in his magical place, and when the time was right he'd figure out the difference all on his own. And if he *did* know the difference, how wonderful that he could so fully inhabit an imaginary world!

Maybe that helps to explain how it was with me and Thor during those days, as I visited him at Uncle Mike's and brought him home. I spun stories about him. I imagined him going with me through my day. I never thought he was *real*, if by real you mean alive, or in some way sentient after death. I just liked to think about him. He was a central character in my life. This didn't trouble me, and it doesn't now. I just liked to imagine he was with me.

The one difference was that I had a physical body that was Thor. It was the same body I'd carried inside me for nine months, and that I'd felt kicking and squirming around for the last four or five of them. It was the same body that had forced its way out of me early in the morning of November 12, 2008. Along the way, it had turned from a living body to a dead body, but it was still Thor. I liked to imagine being with Thor, and this body *was* Thor, so the body became part of my imagining. I never confused Thor's dead body with a living thing, but I also never confused it with something abhorrent. Why should the body that was Thor transmogrify from an intimate member of the family, from an intimate part of my own body, into a repellent object just because it had died? I felt very close to Thor's body.

I was aware that some people might think it was sacrilegious or disrespectful or just gross to carry Thor's body around, to dress it and undress it, to tell it little stories, as if it were a doll. I didn't care what anyone else thought, but some part of my mind was always composing explanations as if to outsiders. Maybe doing that helped me to clarify things to myself, or maybe it just reflected the habits of a professor, always figuring out how to explain things.

When I'd been in the hospital feeling nothing but love for Thor but aware that an outsider looking in might feel uneasy with the sight of someone kissing and rocking and singing to a dead infant, I'd felt the words form in my mind: "I love all my children, whatever their imperfections. Adam is disorganized and sometimes rude and I love him; Thor is dead and I love him." I did that again now. I thought, for the benefit of my imaginary, uncomfortable observer: "Whether or not Glenn and I opt to handle Thor's body, it already has an afterlife that's nothing like your idea of a peaceful corpse lying still and untouched. Organ transplant specialists have removed the heart valves. Forensic physicians have performed an autopsy on it. The staff at the funeral home has embalmed it. After all that, why shouldn't Thor's body also have an afterlife with people who actually loved him? Shouldn't his own parents' hands touch him at least as much as the hands of some doctor or whoever embalmed him?"

And so imagining life with Thor-baby meant living with Thor-body. But the purpose of all this imagining wasn't to have fun adventures as Adam had had with Wolf and his cousins. It was to create memories. Because if we had no memories of

Thor, maybe someday it would be as if he had never existed at all. Certainly no one *else* would carry memories of him. It was going to be entirely up to Glenn and me, so we'd better make sure we had something to remember.

By living with Thor, we could make him exist.

Perhaps the power of the imagination *is* the spiritual.

WHEN WE GOT HOME FROM THE FUNERAL HOME WE discovered that our friends Shel and Ann had sent an email. Their daughter Liz had taken her own life at age 27 a year earlier. They expressed their condolences about Thor, as one pair of grieving parents to another.

Later Glenn and Shel talked. "As horrible as this is," Glenn said, "I can't imagine actually raising a child and *then* having her die."

Shel answered: "But at least people in our situation can be grateful for the time we had with our child, the happy memories. That's what you won't have with Thor."

"*Happy* memories," Glenn said to me that evening. "What a luxury, to be able to specify what kind of memories. We have no memories at all."

I wanted memories. Which meant I wanted experiences. The experiences that would make all those memories.

My scheme to create memories worked. Those visits to the funeral home, those two times when we had Thor at home— that is what I most remember now about those days between his death and the burial. I remember them precisely and sensually: Thor's heft in my arms, his firmly pursed lips, the bend in his elbows as I eased his arms through the sleeves of a new outfit. I remember the places we took him, what Glenn and I said to him, the things we did. I remember happiness, despair, humor, even boredom. The memories are vivid, sharp. I remember those hours with Thor—not more than a few dozen—better than I remember the time without him.

But when I re-read my journals from those days, I'm surprised to see how long we waited before bringing Thor home for the first time. Not till November 20, over a week after his birth and death. In the record of the days before this, I see horror, despondency, doubt, sadness beyond words. Days and hours that stretched like a highway dully bearing straight ahead through a desolate landscape, a highway that had no end, a landscape containing no beauty, no hope, no life.

My entry for November 17 says that that was my worst day yet. Glenn cried because it was all so unfair, and his tears were openly selfish: Why couldn't *he* have a child? He'd wanted one so badly, waited so long, been so deferential to his partners. He didn't say this as an accusation, just as a cry against fate, but on that day I was convinced that it was all my fault, or at least that I had to take the possibility seriously. I had denied Glenn a child. But at least deferential Glenn had been in a position to decide that he would leave the decision about a home birth up to me. Thor had had no voice in the matter, and he was the one who was dead.

We talked about trying again. Glenn had already asked me in the hospital, in four straightforward words: "Should we try again?"

"Yes," I'd said just as simply. It had required no elaboration. I'd gotten pregnant because we wanted a child; that hadn't changed. And I'd only been not-pregnant for a few hours. It was easy to imagine being pregnant again.

But now, on November 17, I was scared. What if we strung along efforts at insemination when there was no point; what if I hadn't been too old a year earlier but now I was? What if I got pregnant and that child had some terrible disability? What if there was another catastrophic delivery?

"Do you remember what you said when we learned that Thor didn't have Down syndrome?" Glenn asked me.

I didn't.

"You said, 'Bad things don't happen to me.'"

Glenn meant to say that I'd be optimistic again; that optimism was my natural state, and that this gloom would pass. But what I said to myself was: "Haha, sucker. You were wrong."

The worst of that day, though, was this: I was beginning to understand what it meant to have days pass without Thor, and to know that more such days stretched ahead, an infinite number. We were supposed to be caring for a newborn. We were supposed to be exhausted with feedings, diaperings, soothings of upset tummies. But now, aside from planning the memorial service, what were we supposed to do with our time? Grade papers? Pick up groceries? The banality of the ways we usually passed our days felt sickening. Hardly anything would change in our routine because of Thor's death, and that felt like a far more vicious violation than having everything change. This was what it meant to experience not the obliteration of a life, but the obliteration of even the possibility of a life.

On that day, when there were no feedings, no diaperings, no baths, no efforts to soothe a crying baby to sleep, even walking the three blocks to the cemetery to pick out a spot for Thor was a relief. At least we were doing something for him.

At some point during that day, my journal tells me, I threw

myself on the living room floor and wailed and pounded my fists. I remember that. I remember not knowing whether I wanted Glenn to discover me and scoop me up and hold me, or whether I wanted for him not to discover me, because I needed to experience some depth of despair on my own, undiluted by someone else's sympathy.

This was the universe of things I might wish for: to have Glenn discover me or not discover me. How laughably small, those options. There was no point wishing for Thor to live.

A couple of days later, I had a dream. I stepped out onto a frozen pond, despite Glenn's warning that the ice might still be thin; winter had just arrived. "Glenn is always overly cautious," I laughed to myself. Then the ice broke and my right leg plunged through, to the thigh. I suddenly felt lost, as if my very being were fading in a space of seconds. I looked back at Glenn with an expression that said, "You'll rescue me, won't you?" I couldn't utter any words, my throat was frozen; all I could do was hope that he could read my face. He looked terribly far away.

Did I want him to rescue me from my despair? Did I want him to have rescued me from my desire for a home birth? Had I become Thor, able only to plead with my eyes because my voice had been struck silent?

The living room where I flung myself to the floor is the darkest room of our house; I've never liked it. It has small windows to the east and north only, and heavy furniture with deep blue upholstery. It has no central lighting, only area lamps. And now it was filled with flowers. Dozens and dozens of bouquets and a few potted plants. The smell was overpowering, choking.

This dark, closed, suffocating room was where we now spent

most of our time. It seemed as though we should sit with the flowers—after all, friends had sent them to mark Thor's death, and Thor's death was what filled our days. When visitors came, we made tea and sat with them in that living room. Later, when we brought Thor home, we set up his portable wicker bassinet on the trunk in the living room, amid the flowers.

Glenn did not scoop me off the floor of the living room, which surely would have irritated me if he'd tried it; the movie cliché that a good hug, a good cry makes a damned bit of difference. He did not pull me out of the ice in my dream, though if that had happened in real life I most definitely would not have been irritated. But that was only a dream.

Here is how he rescued me: By not imagining for a moment that "rescue" was going to be part of this story. By not trying.

No, this is how he rescued me: By coming along for the ride. By setting aside his uneasiness at the idea of making Thor's corpse into our child—of extending our contact with Thor beyond our few hours in the hospital with the Thor who had just been born and died and was still warm and smelled of body, into over a week of intimacy with the Thor who had had tissue removed for donation, who had been autopsied, who smelled of embalming fluid.

Later that day, on the seventeenth, I went to see Thor in the funeral home. Usually Glenn came along, and once Julia came, but this time I went alone.

"Is it OK that I go to see him every day?" I asked Glenn as I reached for my coat, panicking at the thought that a woman who threw herself on the living room floor then comforted herself by going to see her autopsied, embalmed baby—that such a woman might disgust her lover.

Glenn had just finished lunch and was washing the dishes. He put the pot he held into the drying rack, paused, and turned slowly toward me.

"I don't really know what I think about spending time with Thor, as he is at this point," Glenn said in a measured voice, "which is why I don't really feel I have to see him every day." I nodded, dread filling my belly. I was right, he was disgusted.

"But I do know that the only time you're at peace is when you're with him."

No, he wasn't disgusted. He understood. Or he understood that he didn't need to understand.

I nodded dully. Grateful but tired.

As I reached into my purse to pull out my car keys, I saw the light blinking on my phone. I hadn't touched my phone, or even thought about it, since before Thor's birth. I pressed the key for voicemail, and listened.

It was Adam. The message was almost a week old: from the night of November 11, when I'd been in labor.

HEY, THIS is Adam. So, I hear you're in labor, good, good—better you than me—HAHA! Just kidding!

But—listen, seriously, there's something we've got to talk about. That name, Max. Don't do it, I'm telling you, don't do it. I mean, I know it's your grandfather's name and all, and I know about the whole Holocaust thing, but, see, that's the point—you know, your grandfather, um, when was he born, like eighteen eighty something?, and what you gotta think about is the whole kindergarten scene, you know, the first grade scene . . . and I realize that was a little ways back for you, and you might not really remember all the details . . . I mean, don't get me wrong, I'm not saying you're OLD or anything, whoa, whoa, easy there!—all I'm saying is, I think I can remember that stage just a LITTLE better than you can, and that's not the name you want to saddle a kid with.

I don't like it. OK, there, I don't like it, are you happy now? HA HA!

Listen, there are plenty of fine alternatives out there, really, perfectly good names. You and I, we'll just sit down and talk. We'll have a cup of coffee. Just don't do anything rash in the meantime, OK?

Oh, and have a good labor! See ya! Bye!

IT WAS a missive from another planet, the planet of going-to-have-a-baby.

It was like reading European novels from the last years before World War I. They had no idea their world was about to be swept away on the battlefields of Verdun.

A tuft of air hurled itself up from my lungs, through my swollen throat, past my unexpecting tongue and teeth, and escaped into the dark foyer. "Ha."

It was the first time I'd laughed since the stillbirth.

I pulled on my coat and opened the side door—and bright winter light spilled into the house. The sun was shining, and I was going to see Thor.

AFTER I parked the car at the funeral home, I climbed the rear steps and let myself in. I was a regular by now, no need to ring the bell.

Mike brought Thor to me, wrapped in a blanket. "What a cutie. Look at those little lips! He's starting to get a little spot on his cheek, but that shouldn't spread too much since he's in the fridge most of the time. We'll put on a little makeup at the service so he looks nice. Just a little foundation, to cover it up."

Mike had become "Uncle Mike," as in, "Thor, we're going back to Uncle Mike now. He'll take care of you till the next time I visit." Or, "Thor, Uncle Mike put too much cream on your face. Yuck, you're all greasy! I'll wipe some off. But that's OK. Uncle Mike just wants to make sure your skin stays nice."

I took Thor from Mike, turned into the parlor, and closed the door. The room was dark, with heavy shades, patterned wallpaper, and a gas fireplace, though outside there was blinding sunlight. I wanted to take Thor outside, into the living, bright world, into the crisp air, with space far above where we could look up to see the branches of trees leaning over us, bare except for the brown leaves that remained on the oaks, which would stay put till next spring's growth pushed them off. We would do that another day, I knew, the day when I would take Thor home.

But today's visit was inside. I looked at Thor. He was swaddled in a woven white cotton blanket. Only his face peeked out, lips a little pursed, eyes tightly shut, the new bluish spot on his left cheek. I pushed back the blanket from his head, exposed his hair, fine, blond, hardly distinguishable from his skin. The soft spot on the top of his skull, where the bones remained apart in order to compress more easily for the delivery, was sharply visible, a little valley enclosed by three ridges. I pressed my face to his. It was cold and stiff and smelled of formaldehyde. I rubbed my nose against his and smiled: if he were a living baby, a bit older, he'd find this funny.

"Come, Thor, let's look around." I took him to the window and told him how bright it was outside, and how another day we would go outside and take a walk. Then I walked with him around the room, talking him through everything there. That's what I'd done with Adam when he'd been a baby in Berlin.

"Look, Adam, here's the mirror! There's Mommy Lisa in the mirror, and there's Adam, in his red suit. Oh, and look, this is the wallpaper! It's yellow and has a great big rip, right here!" It kept Adam in motion, which he liked, and entertained by my voice.

And so I showed Thor the gaudy porcelain swan that served as the base of a lamp, showed him the glasses turned upside down by the sink, showed him the shelf full of books, with their spines all different sizes and colors.

We sat down on the sofa. I propped Thor on my lap, and we read a book, one of Adam's favorites from when he was small, *Carl's Afternoon in the Park*. It was a board book with no text but with beautiful paintings showing how Carl, a Rottweiler, takes Baby on adventures in the park while Mama goes off to have a cup of coffee with her friend. Carl and Baby go on the merry-go-round, they get cotton candy, they get butted by goats in the petting zoo. Adam had loved the Carl books.

I looked at the pictures with Thor, narrating them and pointing to things like I'd done for Adam. I'd unswaddled Thor by now, so his arms hung visible by his side. When we were done with Carl, I lay Thor down on the sofa beside me. I made a cup of ginger tea in the microwave, pulled out a magazine, and sat back down. With Thor next to me, I sipped my tea, and read.

How can I describe the feeling of having Thor next to me— not speaking to him, holding him, reading to him—just having him next to me as I read and drank tea? I can only describe it this way: it was as it was supposed to be, a few days after his birth, with him sleeping, still and untroubled, and me enjoying both his nearness and the interlude of quiet between feedings, diapering, bouncings. It's fair to ask if one of the great appeals of Thor was that he *was* so quiet, that he made no demands—I could forget the feeling of insanity that goes with having a baby whose crying you can't silence, when nothing works. But in any case, this was the ideal, if you just imagined Thor was sleeping rather than dead. Rather than being a reprieve from his crying, this was a reprieve from his absence.

7

AS THE DAYS PASSED AFTER THOR'S DEATH, I REAL-
ized with horrified wonder that I was doing something I had
never done before, at least not since early childhood. I was having my own experience. No one else's. I was suddenly sharply
aware of how even the most personal moments of our lives are
cluttered by films we've seen, books we've read. Falling in love?
I've watched that movie a thousand times. I know what the
lines are, I know how the soundtrack goes, I know the facial
expressions of the freshly enamored. I have friends who say that
they've missed warning signs coming straight from the mouths
of men they were interested in because they were too busy playing film scripts in their heads.

Discovering you're pregnant. Being reunited with a long-
lost friend. Learning of the death of your child at war. Sitting
at the bedside to say farewell to your terminally ill spouse. I've
seen it all. We all have. There is no way to reclaim an unmedi-
ated experience of these things. Reclaim it? We never had it in
the first place.

But I had no mental images, no script, no soundtrack for
a stillbirth. This was *my* experience, mine to invent, together
with Glenn, and in a way with Mike, who had opened the door
for us to spend those days with Thor.

People used to understand that their family members were

still theirs, even after their deaths. Like in old movies where the body lies in state at home before it's buried. It's even part of our city's architecture. Our old house has two front doors: one to the living room, facing the street, which everyone uses, and one to the dining room, opening sideways onto the porch, which no one uses. The second one was built for taking bodies to the church for the funeral, because you weren't supposed to carry corpses through the front door. Lots of turn-of-the-century houses in our town were built this way: tiny, modest cottages, with only one room for the whole family to sleep in, but with a special door just for dead bodies to exit through.

It is sometimes convenient to be a historian. I don't waste emotional energy worrying about the fact that we're not supposed to caress and carry and adore dead bodies (any more), that we're (now) supposed to keep corpses away from the living. What I know is this: Thor is our child, and he's coming home.

We bring him home, finally, on the twentieth. At the funeral home I take him from Mike's arms into mine, carry him outside—his face exposed to the fresh air, the bright light!—and step into the car, Glenn in the driver's seat, me riding shotgun, Thor in my lap. Thor gets to ride in the Adammobile, crazy art, the kind he surely would have loved, smiley faces and balloons and bubbles and spirals! We drive home, along Gilbert Street, past the Asian food mart where we buy dumplings, past the unfortunately named gas station ("Kum and Go"), past the rec center where Thor and I had done aquacize. The sun is shining, and it feels triumphal: we are bringing Thor home! Right on Washington past the co-op, left on Johnson over the creek, right on Jefferson and into our neighborhood, our neighborhood, we are bringing Thor home to our neighborhood! Past Horace Mann Elementary School, *his* elementary school! Ace Hardware, where the kids buy candy on their way home from school! And across the alleyway from the hardware store: our house, which Adam once said looked like a little village, not a box like the other houses; our house with its crazy extensions and twists and turns and seven different ways to get outside from the ground floor.

This is what I remember, far more than the dismal scenes of Glenn and me in the stuffy living room, which I recall only when I leaf back through my journal. This was my beautiful necrophiliac romance with my baby.

I show Thor his room. I show him where I'd set up the diapering table, all the diapers I'd stacked up for him, the bin for dirty diapers. I tell him how Grandma had found a source for the nicest cloth diapers secondhand. *Grandma likes bargain hunting,* I whisper to him, letting him in on a family joke. I tell him how Grandma had wondered if it was OK to buy pink diapers with flowers, in case he turned out to be a boy, and how I'd said, "I'd rather have a boy than a girl in pink diapers with flowers." Another family joke.

I show Thor the other rooms in the house. I show him Adam's room, so even though Adam is staying at Julia's because he doesn't want to see Thor, Thor can see something of Adam. The clothes strewn about his room, the computer on the desk, the unmade bed, the dishes that haven't been returned to the kitchen. *Adam is kind of messy, Thor, isn't that funny?* I tickle Thor under his chin. *That's just how some kids are.*

This is important. Thor must understand that I love my children even if they aren't perfect.

And Adam loves to do art, I tell Thor, *which is good, because little kids like to do art too.*

I take Thor outside, with Glenn. Glenn, having lost his chance to grow into baby talk, speaks haltingly to Thor, about how glad we are to have him home, how sad we are that he is dead. I, with my greater experience with babies, chatter away about the fallen leaves, the squirrels fattening themselves up for winter, the noisy crows in the trees.

Or: Glenn with no filter enabling him to see Thor as anything other than a corpse, tells him how glad we are to have him home, how sad we are that he is dead. I, determined to believe that there is a child somewhere in that body, chatter away about the fallen leaves, the squirrels fattening themselves up for winter, the noisy crows in the trees.

The backyard. I tell Thor what it would have been like to turn two or three or four, when he would have loved the old goose shed, which would have been his play house. *Adam called it the Dinosaur Clubhouse when he was little,* I tell him. *Maybe later we'll get out some pictures of Adam in the Dinosaur Clubhouse and show them to you.*

We show Thor the garden. *Little children like to see things grow,* I tell Thor. I explain which vegetables little kids especially like, such as carrots, which are crunchy. I explain which animals like to come and visit, like bunnies. *Bunnies eat the lettuce, but they sure are cute, and we like to share with them.*

I pluck some sage from the herb garden and put it into Thor's hand, rubbing it to release the odor. *The sage stays green even when the weather gets cold,* I explain. *We always use it for Thanksgiving dinner, and Thanksgiving is still a week away.* This is good. Thor can see how things grow in the garden, even though most of the vegetables are already gone and he won't be around to see the new crop go in next spring.

We put Thor into a sling and go for a walk. I put on a big coat that drapes over the sling so no one will see that I am carrying a baby and want to take a look. Uncle Mike had suggested this: if you brought home an adult and wanted to go for a walk, he'd said, you'd have to put the body in a wheelchair and the neighbors would definitely wonder about old Aunt Mildred, she didn't look so good all slouched over like that, but with a baby you can take it out under your coat and no one has to know. *Isn't Uncle Mike funny?* I ask Thor. *Doesn't he have good ideas?*

Thor, in his sling. First my secret, then Glenn's; first under my coat, then under Glenn's. Though Glenn carries him only once, then says he doesn't need to do it again. That's all right. I want to carry him myself anyway.

Thor's weight: I feel it in a new way. The pressure of the sling against my back, balancing the pressure of Thor's body in front. Thor pulled close, so even without my arms' help he presses against my breast. My chest compressed, between Thor in the front and the straps of the sling carrying his weight in the back.

It doesn't matter that he's dead. It doesn't matter that he's dead. He's mine. I can carry him around the neighborhood.

We walk to the playground.

Look, Thor, it's the playground! You were here before, when you were really tiny in my tummy, with Rae-Rae and Kiki. And look, there are some of the neighbor kids! They're bigger than you are, so they can slide down the slide and climb up the ladders.

We walk up the brick street to the cemetery, just on the

other side of the playground. There are other children there, too. We tell Thor which ones are close by and how old they got to be and what it was like in the 1950s or 1930s or 1890s when they died. That way Thor will know there are other children who lived and died in a flash just like he did, and that they'll be right nearby.

We show him where he will be buried. We tell him why his plot is special: How it's right next to the woods, so there will be lots of bunnies and squirrels and deer and birds. How there aren't any streetlights, so at night you can see the stars. We tell Thor how we'll dress up the grave with pretty flowers, how we'll put a birdfeeder there to make sure there are lots and lots of bird visitors. We don't want Thor to be lonely. We make sure he understands he won't be alone.

We prepare Thor to go out into his world. Isn't that what you do with your children?

It's true: we have picked out a beautiful spot for Thor's grave. And we look forward to decorating it and to visiting him there—we *look forward* to it. This is the life we will have with our child. It's not all over. It won't be over when we bury him. There is a future. We will visit him and bring birdseed and tell him what's happening at home—home, where he saw his room and Adam's and Mommy's and Daddy's. Home, where he slept.

Where you sleep: that's home. How could our home be Thor's if he'd spent nights in the hospital and at the funeral home, but never at our house?

How could I be the mother of a baby if I'd never fallen asleep as he lay in the bassinet next to our bed?

I bring Thor into bed, prop him up on my lap, read to him. I read the story about the little bunny and big bunny who explain just how much they love each other, and it's always more and more and more. And I tell him that this is just how it is—he loves me and I love him, and I love him so much that I can't even explain how much I love him. Later I will put the book into the casket, with a sprig of sage, so Thor can remember *how Mommy showed me the sage and we smelled it and Mommy read to me and told me how much she loves me, and how we cuddled together and went to sleep. And it was true that Mommy was crying all the while, but that was just because she loves me so much.*

I lay Thor down in the bassinet next to our bed. I stretch my arm over his chest and tummy. I go to sleep, knowing Thor is right there next to me.

In the morning—the morning, when we wake up with our baby, like normal parents!—we dress him. They'd put on a onesie and the pale green cap at Uncle Mike's, but in the meantime we've thought of the clothes that he should be buried in. We've remembered the dark red onesie with the green bird on it, hand sewn by a vendor at the farmer's market. *Julia bought it for you,* I tell Thor. *Julia is your Mommy's friend, Adam's other mother, and she would like for you to be buried in that onesie.* And we put on the cap that Maggie had crocheted for him. *Maggie was excited you were coming,* I tell Thor, *because she liked that Mommy was going to have a baby even though she was older than most pregnant women.*

I once read the memoir of a woman who lived on an island off the west coast of Ireland. Her son, a fisherman, went lost at sea. Days later, his body was found, bloated by the water, with the skull splintered into fragments for having crashed against the rocks of the shore. She washed his body, dressed it, and then laid his head in her lap while she slowly massaged his skull back into a shape that was recognizable, a shape that would allow for a viewing at the wake. All the while she sang to him, spoke to him.

This was her child.

IT'S TRUE that at first Glenn doesn't know whether he wants to bring Thor home. He doesn't know if he wants to carry in a sling a baby whose heart and brain have been removed for the autopsy and who smells like embalming fluid.

But he does know that the only time I am at peace is when I am with Thor.

Glenn believes that it's good that I know what I want, which is to have Thor for many hours in the hospital, not half an hour like the man from the medical examiner's office wanted. To visit Thor at the funeral home. To have Thor come home. It's good that I know what I want and that I make it happen.

Except, what I really want is for Thor to come back to life, and I can't make that happen.

I pull Thor to me as I stand in the breakfast nook, sun streaming in the south-facing windows. I feel his solidity fill my arms, my chest. I lean my cheek against his and whisper, "You're my little Thor, my beautiful Thor, I love you love you love you."

I look at Thor lying on the dark blue sofa in the living room, implacid, unmoving as I stand above him. I stiffen, my mouth clenches, poison runs through my veins. I inhale the thick scent of the flowers. "You little shit," I hiss. "Why are you dead? You little shit."

I hate Thor's deadness.

If I do something with Thor once, I can't do it a second time. It's *boring*. With a live baby it would be fine, because the baby would react differently each time. The first time I show him the kitties, for example, he might fall asleep, and the next time he might get hungry. But with Thor, it's the same each time. I know that live babies are sometimes boring too, that when Adam was a baby I'd sometimes wanted to scream with the tedium of bouncing him for yet another few minutes till he fell asleep. But when Thor bores me it's a reminder that he will never do anything, which is to say that he will never change, which is to say that he will never grow, which is to say that he is dead.

I learn to do everything once, and only once.

Thor bores me, and then he angers me.

He angers me by withholding his voice. "Say something!" I demand threateningly, my eyes trying to bore into him, but he won't be bored into. "Don't just lie there! Get mad! Cry!"

I can see and smell and feel Thor, but I cannot hear him. He doesn't cry. He doesn't whimper. He doesn't sigh. This hadn't occurred to me in the hospital, when I was so busy looking at him and smelling him and touching him that I understood his question about why he was dead without being bothered by the fact that I wasn't *hearing* the question. But now I realize: Thor is perfectly silent. He does not let me hear his cry, or even the tiniest whimper.

He's so remote.

I wonder if voice is the real sign of life, and silence the sign of death.

I wonder if Thor is getting back at the world—at me—in the only way he can, by withholding his voice. Because more than anything else, I want to hear it. And then I think: how dare I demand to hear his voice. He has little enough, he should be able to have his silence, but no, I want to take that from him too.

I understand. Thor does not belong to the funeral home or the hospital, nor is he mine. He belongs to no one but himself.

I admit it, grudgingly.

I admire him.

But his silence will haunt me. When Thor appears in my dreams in the weeks and months to come, he will smile and hold out his arms toward me, but he will not speak or gurgle or cry. Long after he is buried, as I remember his smell and feel and looks, I will long for a memory of his sound. As I write this, my ears search, stretch, twist in an effort to find something, anything, but they still cannot find Thor's voice.

8

"ARE YOU SLEEPING OK?" FRIENDS ASK, EYEBROWS peaked in concern.

Fine, I want to spit back at them. *Just fine. No baby waking up wanting to drink, no pacing around with Thor to soothe his tummy ache, no lying anxiously, wondering if the fact that I haven't heard a sigh from him in the last few minutes means he's stopped breathing. I'm getting plenty of sleep.*

"Fine," I say. "I'm sleeping fine."

I'm also eating well—no meals interrupted by a crying baby—and I'm getting out plenty, untethered to a newborn's unpredictable sleeping and feeding demands.

Why would anybody think that I'd want to sleep well, eat well, get out a lot?

NAOMI LOOKED helplessly into the distance when I saw her with her two-month-old, a few weeks before Thor was due.

"How's the nursing going?" I asked.

She looked past me, eyes awash in despair. "I can't wait to get back to teaching," she said softly. "I feel tethered." And she fell into silence, knowing she was supposed to be happy to breast-feed. That even those three words—I feel tethered—might be construed as a betrayal.

MY MILK comes in on Friday, three days after Thor was born. Soon my breasts are swollen like melons. Rock hard. The skin wants to burst.

Stupid fucking breasts. No one had told them the baby had died. But they should know. How dare they bombard me with milk now.

Beat them back, beat the breasts back. Ice packs. Cabbage leaves. We have a head of cabbage in the basement, leftover from a farmers' market purchase a few weeks earlier. I peel off some dried outside leaves, wrap the rest in a damp towel, and open the fridge door to put the cabbage in. On the shelf at eye level is the leftover salad Glenn had made the night I had gone into labor, the salad we'd eaten after I'd returned from water aerobics. Wilted lettuce, mushy slices of pear, crumbles of cheese, and slivers of meat darkened to a uniform gray by the vinaigrette. With all architectural integrity long gone, the salad sits in a mass in the bottom third of an old yogurt container.

I push the salad back and rest the cabbage in front of it.

I arrange cabbage leaves around my breasts, as the nurses in the hospital had suggested. Each breast takes three or four large leaves. The bra holds them in place. When they go in they're cold. That feels good, and it hurts at the same time. They press against my already swollen breasts, packed into the bra, make everything yet tighter.

This is my nursing bra. It's extra large. Big enough to hold my lactating breasts. But still painfully tight with the cabbage leaves.

When I take off my bra, my breasts have the imprints of the veins in the cabbage leaves. Pretty.

Little ice packs. I have tiny packs, one-by-two inches, clear plastic with some blue substance inside. They came in groups of four, attached to each other, like a string of sausages. I'd used those packs for Adam's school lunches—they were small and could bend, so it was easy to slip them between whatever odd-shaped containers might be jammed into his lunchbox that day.

The little packs are cold on my breasts, and stay cold for a while. Long enough. Then I have to change them, switch back to cabbage leaves.

The breasts must be disciplined. No excuses, no exemptions, no relief. No, I will not pump just a little bit to relieve the pressure. I block from my mind the possibility of pumping in earnest and donating to the milk bank. Someone could use my milk. I don't let myself think about it. Heart valves will have to suffice. Milk must stop. My breasts are too big, too hard.

My belly is too small, too soft. Flat, it is flat. I curl up behind Glenn, dig my fingers into his chest, pull him to me as hard as I can. The last time we lay in bed we couldn't do this: my big pregnant belly was in the way. I draw Glenn closer, wanting his warmth, punishing myself for no longer having the belly. Pull him tighter, pull him tighter, feel, there's nothing there.

We are desperate for each other. Our hands, our mouths, our legs seek to obliterate the space between us.

I lay on top of him. I want to feel him from head to toe, confirm my flatness. I rest my cheek on his cheek, my chest on his chest, my belly on his belly, my thighs on his thighs, my feet on his ankles. He is flat, I am flat. We are two planes, and so we can come together. Three nights ago I was not a plane. Three nights ago I had three dimensions: top to bottom, left to right, and front to back. Now front to back is in the funeral home.

"OH, *MAN*!" Caroline shook her head, wry smile on her face. The new veteran of childbirth, the new teller of war stories, the new member of the club. "That epidural, that was some sweet shit. Hell, I was so ready for it. One minute killer pain, the next minute nothing." Nellie lay on her lap, less than a week old, and Caroline fingered her hair.

"Then they decided for a C-section, just a few minutes later, Nellie's heart had actually stopped. Freakiest feeling ever, they pumped me up with local anesthetic, I was wide awake but didn't feel the cut—just the sudden release of all that pressure. One minute, that tight, tight belly, then—kapow!—everything let go. Like popping a big old zit."

MY BELLY is flat.

LIE ON him, lie on Glenn. Feel the absence. Press your chest, your belly, your thighs against his. Feel his whole body with your whole body. Punish yourself. You could not do this three days ago. Now you do it for comfort. How dare you.

I roll over, bringing Glenn with me. He lies on top. We haven't lain this way for months. He compresses my flatness, makes it even flatter. See, there's nothing there. I am two dimensional. I want him to press me flatter, flatter, make me truly two dimensional. I have no business being here under him, comforted by his weight. My belly is too small, too soft.

My breasts are too large, too hard. You feel sore, breasts? Your own damned fault. Here, let me give you a cabbage leaf, and another, and another. Big, thick cabbage leaves. Suffocating. I layer them on you. You can't breathe, you say? Good, I'll put on another. Damn you, no one wants your milk. If you insist on producing it anyway, you can pay, you can live with the pain. I will smother you, and soon you won't produce any more. You will shrink, wither, skulk away, retreat into yourselves. You will learn your lesson.

They shrink, wither, skulk, retreat. They obey meekly and perfectly, like a puppy who turns back, tail between its legs, as soon as its owner speaks to it in a tone that indicates that no nonsense will be tolerated.

A week after Thor's birthday, it's all over; my breasts are defeated. That last little bit of possibility, the echo of the fact that a baby was born and babies get hungry and so mothers produce food for them. My breasts had believed Thor was alive and behaved as if he were, and if they believed it, would that make it so? The light we see of a star that died a hundred million years ago, because it takes that long for the light to reach us.

A week after that we make love. My belly is too small, too soft. Flat. I lie under Glenn, wanting to be pressed into the bed. Glenn on top of me, Glenn inside me, Glenn around me, obliterating the space where Thor was, erasing it. I bleed a little, but not much. The doctors had said to wait six weeks, but we cannot wait, we need each other too much, and my body had disposed of Thor in two weeks anyway.

Squeeze me, squeeze me. Squeeze my breasts, it doesn't

hurt, the milk is gone. My belly, flatten it more, for it is already flat. Its insides are in the funeral home. Press me. I draw Glenn toward me for comfort. I draw him toward me as punishment, for I should not be able to lie flat against him. My third dimension is in the funeral home. I have expelled it, and it is in the funeral home. I seek comfort by pressing the baby's absence against my lover. How dare I.

9

EVEN WHEN WE WEREN'T VISITING THOR, WHEN WE
didn't have him home, Glenn and I filled our days with him.
We were supposed to be occupied with a newborn. Caring for
a newborn is a full-time job. Glenn tended the dozens of bouquets that filled our dark living room with the sweet, choking
odor that seemed appropriate to our choking throats. I wrote
about Thor in my journal.

But mainly, we planned the memorial service in meticu-
lous, time-consuming detail. Glenn pored over music that
made him think of Thor and burned a CD to play during the
visitation, an hour before the service. Glenn and I both prepared statements for the service. We talked to Shel and Ann,
whose service for their daughter had moved us, asked my sister to play bassoon and my brother to officiate, and let others
know that they would be free to speak if they liked.

We chose photos for the bulletin board that would stand
outside the hall. Here the three of us in the hospital, Thor
between us, Glenn kissing his brow as I rest my finger inside
Thor's curled fist. Here Thor and I, still in the hospital, facing each other, my hands holding him upright, my eyebrows
peaked and mouth open to talk to Thor, Thor's head tilted
questioningly to the side. Here Glenn standing up, cradling
Thor in his arms, looking down at him, biting his lip, unable

to speak. Thor on my lap at home, now wearing the deep red onesie with the green bird, both of us facing the camera, my head rested on his, my hand helping his to wave for the camera. Thor lying in his bassinet, eyes closed as if asleep, a green, plush frog keeping him company, both of them covered by the pastel patchwork blanket our friends Cathy and Omar had given us in anticipation of Thor's birth.

I searched through books looking for verses to put in the program. I read the Icelandic Edda, the thirteenth-century prose and poetry cycle that describes Thor and the other Norse gods. I couldn't find a single passage that, even taken out of context, suggested anything other than violence and vengeance. But Julia's mother had included in her email to us a passage from Goethe that Glenn always returned to, and I remembered that Toni Morrison's *Beloved* was all about being haunted by a lost baby. I found a few lines in which Beloved's mother insisted that she *was* her child's mother, that the child's death didn't change a thing.

I designed the funeral program and wrote Thor's biography for the last page. Glenn wanted an open casket to show that Thor existed; I wanted a biography to show that he had lived. That he had visited Lucerne and Vienna and Budapest and Copenhagen and Wyoming and the East Coast. That he had liked walking and swimming, but not so much sitting still.

The biography went above a picture Glenn had taken in the hospital of Thor from behind, my hands propping him up on my lap, his upright head, which obscured my face, perched confidently atop his thick, sturdy back, which in its turn was anchored by hips and buttocks that vanished into the sheet. On this picture, no tubes or pins or tape showed: just a solid body, tinged a little purple from the oxygen-hungry blood that still inhabited his veins. Thor faced away from the camera, and although I knew that when the picture had been taken I'd been smiling at him and he'd been looking dumbly at me, on the program it looked as though he had turned his back on whomever wanted to see him through the camera's lens, as though he had already said goodbye.

10

ONE DAY, WHEN ADAM AND I WERE IN THE LIVING room of our Toledo apartment—he was in first grade, and we hadn't yet moved to Iowa City—I could tell that he was getting into his storytelling mood. But he surprised me. He didn't suggest that we tell about Wolf and his cousins. He said, "Let's tell about Eagle Baby and Eagle Mama in their nest."

"Sure," I said. "Do you want to take a walk while we tell?" He did, and so we put on our jackets and headed north on Robinwood Street, where we lived, then turned right on Central Avenue, which marked the border of our little neighborhood. It was fall, and the big, old maples were turning yellow and orange.

I don't remember any details about Eagle Baby and Eagle Mama in their nest. I just remember that, somewhere on Central Avenue, I realized that Eagle Mama was going to die before the walk was over. Nothing like this had ever happened in one of Adam's stories. There were no explicit hints—Eagle Mama wasn't sick, for example. I just had a feeling that she was going to die. But Adam kept telling the story, untroubled, and I kept adding a few words when he indicated that it was my turn. Neutral words, like "And then what did Eagle Baby say?" I didn't want to direct this story; I wanted to see where Adam took it.

And so we told the story, down Parkwood Avenue, by the back of Rosary Cathedral, in whose parking lot Adam had learned to ride a bike, past the big Victorian house where the landlords of our previous apartment lived. We told as we went along tiny Winthrop Street, where the grandmother of Adam's friend Ibrahim lived, and south on Scottwood, where my friends Nora and Bobby lived with their two cats. The story got more serious—I remember the mood, even though I don't remember the story. There was no clear information to suggest that Eagle Mama was headed toward a bad end. But the mood was enough.

Suddenly, Adam stopped in his tracks and burst into tears.

"Why are you crying?" I asked.

"Because Eagle Mama is going to die!" he said, sniffing and gasping for breath.

I looked down at him. "She is, really?" I asked.

"Yes, she's going to die, and Eagle Baby is going to be all alone, and he'll be so sad!"

"Oh, Adam, that's terrible!" I said. "Why is she going to die?"

"I don't know yet," he sniffed. "I just know she's going to."

And then he started walking again and went back to telling the story. Adam told the rest of it through tears, but he had no power to change its trajectory, to save Eagle Mama. Nor did he have the power *not* to tell the story to its end. Eagle Mama died.

We never returned to Eagle Mama and Eagle Baby. The story was over. The next time Adam was in a storytelling mood, he wanted to tell of Wolf and his cousins.

Then one spring day a year and a half later, when Adam

was nearing the end of second grade, we told of Wolf and his cousins as we drove to the supermarket. As we headed south on Summit Street, in Iowa City, where we now lived, Adam uttered some line about Wolf and his cousins, and then said, "All right, I'm done."

I felt a flash of dizziness and gripped the steering wheel of the car whose paint job lay years in the future. Adam didn't mean he was done telling stories for this drive, he meant he was *done*. In a burst I saw a whole era of his childhood quietly slip away, not with a whimper or with embarrassment at its immaturity, but with the simple dignity of knowing that it had completed its task. I turned left onto Burlington and said a silent goodbye to Wolf, his cousins, and the Adam who had inhabited their world. And I wondered what wonders the next Adam would bring.

I DIDN'T want my family and Glenn's to come. They were coming to take Thor away from me. They were coming to bury him.

On the morning when they were to arrive, our friends Jacki and Patty came to prepare our house for us. They attacked with a fury I've never managed to muster for cleaning. They scrubbed the floors and vacuumed the carpet. They removed the rug from under the dining room table, took it outside, and beat it. I locked myself in the laundry room and folded clean clothes and doubled over with screaming sobs.

After Jacki and Patty left, we picked up Thor from Uncle Mike's, and we took him for a walk. It was cold, and the loose wool coat I'd borrowed from Julia didn't lend much warmth. But it draped easily over Thor in his sling, and so I could carry him hidden. The knowledge that we were marking time left us with little to say. Once we got back home, it would be to the noise and clutter of our families.

Glenn and I had both been to City Park a thousand times, for summer theater, for runs, for picnics. And so we were surprised to find something we'd never noticed before: a bronze statue of an angel on the lawn between the river and the merry-go-round. It was my height and had the kind of neutral, delicate-featured face that revealed that the sculptor thought of angels as white prepubescent children; and it had out-stretched wings, the right one lower than the left. On the inside of the right wing, the word "HOPE" was carved. On the back of the base was a plaque that announced a gathering for lost babies—miscarriages, stillbirths, and infant deaths—at seven p.m. on December 6. No year: this was apparently an annual gathering.

Glenn was struck by the coincidence of our discovering the statue as we took our last walk with Thor. He wanted to attend the ceremony, and so we did, three weeks later. It was thickly dark, with temperatures in the single digits. Visitors placed votive lights in pink (girl), blue (boy), or purple (unknown, and Thor) bags at the base of the statue, where the cutting wind extinguished many of them. The electric system that lighted the podium and powered the microphone went on and off at will. Some thirty people grasped paper cups of hot chocolate and listened as others read poems and sang songs to their children, voices breaking through tears.

Speakers cried as they described the miscarriages and still-births they'd had years earlier, but which still haunted them. Many of the people clearly knew each other; they spoke often of their church communities. The organizer, with whom we spoke afterward, explained that he had never lost a child, but he had lost control of his car a few years earlier and killed a nineteen-year-old university student who was driving in the opposing lane. This event was his way of commemorating her and acknowledging her parents' grief, together with the grief of all parents who have lost children.

It was like observing someone else's very moving ritual. Angels did nothing for us. We collected our free copy of the book-after-the-Hallmark-Channel-movie that had inspired the Angels of Hope movement—there are such statues in dozens of cities, we learned, and they all host a ceremony on December 6—and went back home. I wondered when the statue had been installed and found online the minutes of the City Council debate a couple of years earlier. All the City Councilors had been very sympathetic to parents' grief, but some had worried about the installation of a statue with a religious symbol on city property. The organizers had assured the City Council that this was a non-sectarian, non-faith-based angel.

The next year, I wanted to attend the service and read some of my own writings about Thor. Many of those attending were comforted by thoughts of angels, I thought, but maybe there was also a place for the screaming horror and bitterness that came with being pretty sure that your baby was just *dead*. But the next year, the service was moved to a church; no one wanted to risk frostbite again. Glenn and I didn't feel we belonged, and even if the organizers had said "of course you're welcome to come!" which is exactly what they would have said if they'd known of our hesitation, we knew we'd feel out of place. So we didn't go.

That was all later. On that last evening before Thor's burial we all had dinner together: my parents, Glenn's parents and sister, and Adam. My sister and brother would arrive the next day. Glenn's family and mine had never met. It was like a wedding, only it was a funeral.

Glenn and I had planned the memorial service to the finest detail. But we had forgotten to plan the graveside service, which followed the public service and which was for the family only. Mike drove us from the public service to the cemetery in his van—no need for a hearse for a little baby, he had said. Glenn sat in the front seat with Mike. I sat in the back next to Thor, who lay in the raw pine coffin that Glenn had finished with tung oil. Adam had painted the lid with a peaceful fetus, deep blue with white outlined features, against a splattered red background.

Glenn and I had thought of only two things for the graveside service: that Adam and Julia would hold one strap, and Glenn and I the other, to lower Thor's casket into the grave, and that we would toss clumps of soil from the Dinosaur Clubhouse into the grave. And so, when we all climbed out of our cars near the gravesite, all I could do was look at the expectant faces of my family and Glenn's and say, "We didn't think of anything to say here. I guess we should just bury him."

We lowered Thor's casket into the grave and poured handfuls of earth onto it. The soil bounced and skittered across the lid Adam had painted, slowly covering the image of the fetus that looked westward, toward our house. My parents and brother and sister reached into the ivory-colored plastic pail for their own handfuls of dirt. Glenn's family, unfamiliar with this Jewish tradition and protective of Glenn's stepfather

Marlin, who might easily have slipped on the sloping, uneven lawn leading from the road down to the ravine where Thor's grave lay, stayed back, toward the road, and so they most easily reached their car when I nodded that it was over.

My brother had to leave early the next morning, but the rest of our families stayed through Thanksgiving. The day after the burial, we went to the John Deere Museum an hour away in Moline. Marlin liked mechanical things, Glenn had said; he would enjoy the museum. But Marlin was having trouble breathing and so he sat on a chair tucked into the corner for most of our stay at the museum. I pulled a chair to an exhibit I found interesting, but the guard told me I wasn't allowed to do that: the chairs had to stay in their places. I didn't want to tell her that I was tired from having delivered a baby less than two weeks ago and having buried him yesterday, so I rose and let her take the chair without a word.

Later, a different guard, a chatty one, engaged us in conversation. "Look at that little girl over there," she said, shaking her loose, brown curls and gesturing across the room. The little girl had stringy, blonde hair and a tube in her throat. "Sad, sad," the guard said. Glenn and I looked each other, and Glenn's eyes said, "She's alive; she's four years old and climbing on the tractors at the John Deere Museum." The guard discovered that we were an extended family and volunteered to take pictures of us in front of the tractors, but when we looked at the pictures later we discovered they were backlit and our faces invisible.

On Monday following Thanksgiving I drove my sister to the airport. She was the last to leave. Winter had arrived overnight and we stepped outside that morning to a killing cold. We wrapped scarves around our faces and walked headlong into a wind that seared like sandpaper. The thermometer read fifteen degrees; the wind chill was probably below zero.

Up until this moment, I had been able to imagine that Thor was a baby in a bucolic spot, embraced by oaks, with deer visiting at dusk and birds darting and dipping from the trees down to the bushes behind Thor's grave that still held a few shriveled blackberries. But this was different. Human beings could not survive in this environment. They had to seek shelter. So too did the deer and the birds, who remained huddled in their hollows or nests.

But for Thor it was all the same; he didn't care. He could be in the earth that would freeze in the next days before being coated by a blanket of snow. He wouldn't mind that the snow would develop an icy crust over the course of the winter and then drip frigid water into the sodden earth—into his grave— with the spring thaw. Thor was not one of us. He was just a frozen, autopsied, embalmed, and indifferent corpse.

IV

War Guilt

I WANTED TO WRITE BARB FROM FAMILY PRACTICE A
card, to let her know how important that conversation had
been, the one where she'd asked me how I'd feel if I had a home
birth and something happened. She beat me to it. She phoned
on my third day back home from the hospital, while I was eating breakfast.

"Lisa, I saw the obituary, I am so, so sorry."

It took me a moment to adjust to the thought of talking to
her. Glenn had been the one to pick up the phone, and he'd
passed it to me, hand covering the mouthpiece, whispering,
"*It's Barb.*"

I took a breath.

"Thanks, Barb. It's good of you to call."

"I'm just—so stunned. I can't imagine what this is like for
you."

I looked out the window at the garden I'd abandoned halfway through the summer. "It's terrible. It's unreal. I don't know
if I've fully wrapped my mind around it."

"What happened?"

"It looks like it was a sudden placental abruption, during
labor. Everything was fine going into labor—baby had a strong
heartbeat, everything was just fine. My last prenatal appointment, the day before, was fine too. At least, that's what the

midwife suspects, placental abruption. There'll be an autopsy, so the official cause of death will come in a few weeks."

"Did the doctors say anything?"

"No, by the time I got to the hospital, it was all over . . ." I stopped. "Did you know that I ended up doing a home birth?" I hadn't seen Barb or talked to her since that phone call. I didn't know if she'd looked at my medical records, which would show that I'd gotten prenatal care from the midwives' clinic for several months but then stopped, which might show I'd raised the issue of home birth in my last appointment with the midwives in September.

There was a moment of silence. "No, I didn't know."

"And Barb, ever since it happened, I've wanted to write you a card, to tell you how incredibly important that phone conversation was, where you talked about your niece. You're the one person who asked that question—how would I feel if something happened? If it weren't for that, I'd be completely blindsided now, I honestly wouldn't have given it a moment's thought, it wouldn't have occurred to me to ask myself that question."

"Oh, Lisa."

"I mean, I went ahead and did it anyway, because I saw what you were saying as personal advice, not medical advice . . . you weren't really talking about medical reasons why I should or shouldn't do it, so I ended up talking to the midwives in the clinic, and they basically said: 'We're hospital people, we're more comfortable with hospital births, but you're low risk, you're the kind of person who can do a home birth.'"

"They said that?"

"Yes, they said that." I wanted her to know that I'd sought

out medical advice, and had listened to it. "And that was fine, I think they were right—I was low risk. But now—now it really helps that I was forced to think about how I'd feel if something went wrong. Or . . . even if we didn't really think about it, which we didn't, at least the question was put out there."

"Oh gosh, Lisa, I don't know what to say. I wouldn't have advised you to do a home birth, you know that. But if that conversation was helpful, then I'm glad."

"It was. I don't know that it would have gone any differently in the hospital. Basically, I was so early in labor, I was at the stage where, even if I'd been doing a hospital birth, I wouldn't have been in the hospital yet. The contractions were mild, short—the kind where they say, wait at home a while, no need to come in at this stage. And then all of a sudden I started bleeding, and things just moved incredibly quickly. I don't know if it would have made a difference if I'd been planning a hospital birth."

"It's true, with some of these cases you just can't know if anything could have been done. But that doesn't make it any easier. How are you doing, physically?"

"Fine. I didn't have any hemorrhaging or anything. I left the hospital the same day—they wanted to keep me another night, but I didn't want to, so they did a round of tests, blood pressure, iron level, whatever, and said it was fine if I went home. I spent yesterday running errands."

"You spent *yesterday* running errands?"

This part always made me cry, even months later when I'd tell it. "Yes. It seems really perverse. I'm so strong, the pregnancy was so easy, I was so fit through the whole thing, I'm bouncing around two days later, and Thor was so vulnerable.

I feel like . . . I don't need all this strength, I would have been happy to give him some of mine."

Barb sighed. "So, what do they recommend for follow-up?"

"They said I should just do the usual six-week postpartum visit."

"You'll do that with them, in OB-GYN?"

"They said I could do it there, or with you, it's my choice. I'd rather just come see you. You know me better than they do." I stirred my coffee, which was growing cold.

"Sure, that would be fine. Call me before then if I can do anything."

"OK, I will."

"And take care of yourself. Do you have people to help you out?"

"Yeah, the history department is like a well-oiled grieving machine. We've had way too many of these kinds of things in the last couple of years. They jump into action, food deliveries, cleaning, whatever's helpful."

"Well, I'm glad to hear that. Again, call if you need anything, or if you'd like to see me earlier."

"I will. Thanks. Thanks for calling."

I hung up and looked at Glenn. "I guess I don't need to write that card now."

He gave a half-ironic shrug. "That was nice of her to call. Had she heard through the hospital?"

"No, she saw the obituary in today's paper."

"Oh." Glenn looked down, then looked back up. He let out a breath. "I guess this means it's really public now. Whoever we missed with our mass emails yesterday will know about it."

"Yeah. Who knows who we'll hear from now."

But Barb was the only one who called after reading the obituary. Everyone else sent emails or a card.

I NEXT saw Barb at my annual physical, a year after the physical where she'd confirmed I was pregnant.

"How are you doing?" Barb asked. She sat at her desk, chair turned outward to face me as I sat in one of the three chairs that leaned against the wall next to the desk. We'd sat this way a couple of times a year for ten years.

"Up and down. Fine physically. I ended up going to OB-GYN for my postpartum visit so I could ask them some things. I'm in totally fine physical shape."

"You're such a healthy person," she sighed. "Are you eating OK, sleeping OK?"

"Yeah, all that's fine."

"Are you getting exercise?"

"Yes, I run when it's nice out, but that doesn't happen much in February, so I go to the gym otherwise. I still go to aquacize sometimes—it's a nice group of people."

"Right, you said you were doing that during the pregnancy. So you're back at it again?"

"Mainly as a social thing. It was perfect when I was very, very pregnant, which means it's nowhere near enough of a workout now. I can't get my heart rate up no matter how hard I try. But it's a really great bunch of women; they've been incredibly supportive. So I go there once in a while. It's good."

Barb cocked her head. "Doesn't Deanne Wortman teach some of those classes?"

"Yeah, she's the best. *She* gives a real workout."

"That's good that you're still going there, that's a wonderful place to get support."

Later, when I was checking out, I saw that Barb had checked the boxes on the billing form for annual physical, Pap smear—and grief counseling. She spent a lot of time with me.

After my Pap smear, when I was dressed again, she continued.

"I don't know, this must all be so hard. Especially in your situation, where you can't just keep trying. This kind of thing never goes away, but for younger women who go on to have a child, that does help balance it out a little."

"Oh, we're going to try again."

Barb looked up, startled.

"I talked to the people at OB-GYN about it. As far as they're concerned, Glenn and I are obviously still fertile, my uterus is perfectly capable of carrying a baby to term, and what happened last time had nothing to do with my age—it was just one of those things. They don't see me as being at particular risk for another placental abruption."

Barb put down her pen, speechless.

"Apparently if you have a placental abruption, they worry about a recurrence in subsequent pregnancies starting about two weeks before the stage where you had your first one," I explained. "So if you had a placental abruption at thirty weeks, they consider you at risk as of twenty-eight weeks. But I was twelve days postdate, so they basically just say: don't let it go postdate. Or maybe consider induction a little earlier. The guy I saw said he'd suggest inducing at thirty-eight weeks. I'm not sure that's really necessary; that's like four weeks before when it happened this time around, and induction has its own problems . . . but I figure that's the kind of thing we can discuss if and when I get pregnant again, when they can see how it's going. We don't have to decide that in the abstract."

Barb let out a breath. "So, you'll try again."

"Yes. I got pregnant because we wanted a kid. That hasn't changed. If we were a little younger, we'd probably wait a while, just to work through the stillbirth first. But that's a luxury we don't have. So we just have to go into this knowing it'll be emotionally complicated."

"I really wasn't expecting that. But if you want to, then of course you should. You *are* incredibly healthy and you did have a very good pregnancy."

"We want to."

"Well, you're obviously talking to OB-GYN about this. Just follow the medical advice."

"Of course."

She looked sternly at me. "*All* the medical advice."

I froze.

"Not like last time, when you didn't listen to me and your baby died," is what I heard.

Now I understood. The question wasn't just how I would feel having chosen a home birth if the baby died. The question was what everyone else would think of me.

I knew this already, really. I'd known it since four days after the stillbirth, when a friend who had lived until recently under a repressive regime had brought by a vegetable pie, accepted Glenn's offer of tea, sat down, stretched out his arms in an enormous yawn, and sighed, "Ah, yes, this American do-it-yourself mentality. It brings a lot, but let me tell you, when it comes to things like education and health care, there's something to be said for societies where the authorities retain their authority."

No. I'd known it since the day after the stillbirth, when Julia had told me an obstetrician friend who lives in a different time zone and had never met me had declared, "She had no business having a home birth," without bothering to find out even the most basic information about what had actually happened.

I already knew that people who knew none of the particulars of my pregnancy and stillbirth, who had friends or relatives who had had stillbirths in hospitals, would nevertheless assume that the home birth was to blame, and so I was to blame.

But I hadn't expected it from Barb.

$$2$$

ALL THE ADVICE BOOKS AND LISTSERVS SAID THE same thing: *Don't torture yourself with questions about whether it was anything you did. Whether you shouldn't have continued lifting your toddler in your last trimester, whether you shouldn't have had that wine before you even knew you were pregnant. Almost surely, it was nothing you did. The truth is, you'll probably never know for sure what caused the stillbirth. For 60 percent of stillbirths, the official cause is "unknown." Even the doctors don't know. Don't torture yourself.*

"Don't worry your pretty little head about it," I mocked.

"Not good enough," I spat.

You'll never know for sure comes after you try to find the answers. Not as a way to prevent you from asking the questions.

Awaiting the funeral, my mother asked, eyes churning, what everyone else was too polite to ask. What most people found it unnecessary to ask, since of course the answer must be "yes."

Would it have turned out differently if it hadn't been a home birth?

"No," I said, and told her what Deirdre had told us when she had visited in the hospital. I had had a sudden placental abruption. Placental abruption means the baby stops getting oxygen. The baby tries to breathe—its lungs are mature—but gets only meconium. No oxygen to the brain: four minutes till severe brain damage, six minutes till death. Hospital standard for a C-section is thirty minutes decision-to-incision. Even an emergency C-section wouldn't have been fast enough.

I had my answer.

But I kept asking.

This was a research question. It was a job for my analytic mind, which retreated periodically in those days to make room for my screaming and wailing mind, but which never wandered very far off. It was good at what it did.

As my milk came in, the milk no one wanted, I clicked open my laptop, went to the search engines of the university's medical library, and typed: *stillbirth.*

The glowing computer screen informed me: *The medical community doesn't know much about stillbirths. They haven't attracted much attention. Data collection is inconsistent from state to state, but a common estimate is one stillbirth per 115 live births in the United States. There are roughly ten times as many stillbirths annually as there are cases of sudden infant death syndrome (SIDS). Yet there are extensive public awareness campaigns concerning SIDS, while stillbirth has attracted very little attention from the medical community and the public is generally ignorant of it.*

I continued to type. More information, please, about *placental abruption.* The glowing computer screen told me that *placental abruption is one of the major causes of stillbirths.*

And that was about all.

The studies lumped together all types of placental abruptions: *those that occur as early as twenty weeks, those that occur when the fetus is viable, and those that occur when labor has already begun; complete placental abruption, in which the placenta separates fully from the uterine wall and the oxygen flow to the fetus is cut off, and partial placental abruption, in which only a portion separates and the oxygen flow is slowed but not halted.*

Their findings were limited to a tallying of outcomes: *how many abruptions led to death, how many to severe disability, and how many to birth of a healthy infant.*

The research didn't explore causes, prevention, or treatment. Instead, it focused on risk factors and detection.

Placental abruption has known risk factors. The major ones are smoking, gestational diabetes, cocaine use, and prior history of placental abruption.

None of these applied to me.

Secondary risk factors include advanced maternal age.

That applied to me.

Indications that a placental abruption might have occurred include slowed fetal heartbeat and reduced fetal activity due to reduced oxygen flow. These can be detected by nonstress tests.

Once I'd gone past my due date of October 30, I'd had nonstress tests every other day. Heartbeat and fetal movement had been consistently good. My placental abruption had almost certainly occurred during labor.

If the nonstress tests indicate a possible problem, or if the woman is a week postdate, an ultrasound is usually ordered.

I didn't have an ultrasound when I went postdate. Had I been receiving my prenatal care in the hospital, the staff would probably have ordered an ultrasound.

An ultrasound can confirm some, but not all, placental abruptions, because some placental abruptions are hidden from view by the fetus. Furthermore, ultrasounds only detect placental abruptions that have already occurred; they do not detect weaknesses that might lead to an abruption in the future, eg, during labor.

I had my answer. An ultrasound wouldn't have detected anything anyway.

BUT IN DECEMBER, as I reached for one Christmas cookie after another, my glowing computer screen also delivered this information about *C-sections*: *The thirty minute decision-to-incision guideline,* which Deirdre had mentioned in the hospital, turned out to be a *target suggested by the American College of Obstetrics and Gynecology, aimed at hospitals that do not yet move this quickly. Many hospitals perform C-sections much more quickly, some as quickly as five minutes.*

My glowing computer screen had nothing to say about my hospital, but I inferred: because my hospital is a major teaching hospital, it probably falls into that class of hospitals that move quickly in emergency cases.

I had my answer. If I'd been in the hospital, I'd have had a C-section.

BUT THAT LEFT OPEN THE QUESTION of whether I'd have been in the hospital when the abruption occurred, even if I'd been planning a hospital delivery.

In January, as we cleared away the last of the well-wishers' flowers, I blew away the dust that had gathered on my abandoned pile of pregnancy guides and refreshed my memory on the subject of *hospital standards regarding when a laboring woman should come in.*

Hospitals advise against coming in as soon as you're in labor.

It's likely to take many hours, and there's no need for medical involvement in the early stages of labor. You'll be more comfortable at home, and the hospital prefers to keep the beds open for women who are closer to delivery.

I inferred: if I'd called the hospital and told them I was having mild contractions of twenty-five to thirty seconds, they would have told me not to come in yet.

I had my answer. I wouldn't have been in the hospital anyway.

STILL, I HAD TO CONSIDER the fact that those early contractions, weak and short as they were, were close together— every five to seven minutes, instead of the twenty minutes or more one might expect in early labor. Perhaps this would have been enough to make the hospital suggest I come in just to be on the safe side. At that point, they would have discovered that I was no more dilated than I had been the day before, they would have witnessed how mild the contractions were, and they would have heard a strong fetal heartbeat. They might have interpreted this as Deirdre had: labor had begun, but it would be a while. They might have suggested I go back home to wait it out, since I live less than a ten-minute car ride away. But once in the hospital, given the frequency of the contractions, they might have suggested I just stay.

I had my answer. Maybe I'd have been in the hospital. Or maybe not.

THOUGH PERHAPS NONE OF THIS WAS RELEVANT, because there was also this: in February, after I'd begun going to water aerobics again, I had an appointment at the reproductive endocrinology clinic. The purpose of the appointment was to see if a future pregnancy would be dangerous. And so I asked about *prior history of placental abruption as a risk for subsequent pregnancies.*

The pale doctor who avoided eye contact informed me that *my placental abruption did not put me at elevated risk of another placental abruption. Placental abruptions tend to happen at roughly the same stage of pregnancy in the same woman. My abruption occurred during labor. I was eleven days postdate when I went into labor, twelve days when Thor was born.*

And so the risk could be avoided by *induction.*

The pale doctor who avoided eye contact informed me that *he would suggest that I not let a subsequent pregnancy go postdate. In fact, he would suggest that I induce at thirty-eight weeks.*

I didn't like the idea of planning an induction two weeks ahead of due date—four weeks ahead of my last abruption, at a gestational stage associated with a greatly elevated incidence of subsequent problems for babies born so early—prior to even getting pregnant. It was this kind of thinking that had made me want to work with midwives rather than obstetricians in the first place.

I didn't want to discuss with this doctor how to proceed in a hypothetical future pregnancy. He clearly didn't think much of the forty-six-year-old woman who had chosen a home birth.

He avoided my eyes.

He looked at my chart.

Someone had noted there that I'd had a home birth with a "lay midwife." This wasn't true. Deirdre was a certified nurse-midwife.

The pale doctor who avoided eye contact was part of the same team that didn't know the difference between direct-entry midwives and certified nurse-midwives. The team that used the derogatory term "lay midwife" for direct-entry midwives.

It wasn't necessary to resolve the question of a future induction with him. If I had another pregnancy, he wouldn't be the one to monitor it. I could discuss induction with my midwives or doctors late in the pregnancy, when we could consider not only my prior history but also how things were going with the current pregnancy.

The pale doctor who avoided eye contact was no longer talking about a future pregnancy. He was talking about the pregnancy just past. *He never would have let my pregnancy go on as long as it had. Even without a prior history of placental abruptions, the hospital would have scheduled induction when I was a week postdate.*

I had my answer. I'd have been induced.

THOUGH I COULDN'T HELP RECALLING that I knew two women who had given birth in this hospital and gone postdate. They'd been scheduled for induction when they were ten days, not seven, postdate. Ten days was only one short of my eleven, suggesting that the hospital might have seen my eleven-day-postdate pregnancy not wildly, irresponsibly postdate, but only barely beyond the point where they would have taken action.

Still, even an induction at ten days would have been an induction.

I had my answer. I'd have been induced.

THOUGH I SUSPECTED that the same might have happened with the Berlin midwives' practice, or with other midwives working in friendlier conditions. Less isolated and better able to consult with peer midwives as well as cooperative obstetricians, they might have made a different judgment call regarding my postdate pregnancy and, after a week, referred me to a hospital for additional tests or possible induction.

THOUGH TO FURTHER COMPLICATE THINGS, as Glenn pointed out, there was the possibility that I might not have gone along. The pale doctor who avoided eye contact said he would have ordered induction, but he wouldn't have had the power to schedule one. He could have recommended an induction. He assumed that if he recommended it, I would have had it.

But I might have declined.

Keeping in mind that all medical procedures carry risks, and that induction frequently leads to a need for further, more serious, interventions, I would have wanted it demonstrated to me that the risks of induction were less than the risks of letting the pregnancy continue, if there was no indication from nonstress tests and other diagnostic tools that the pregnancy was in danger.

"You wouldn't have agreed," Glenn said. "You'd have pushed back."

AND FOR THAT MATTER, I would also have recalled that sometimes pregnancies are considered postdate when they really aren't. Flipping through the pages of my pregnancy guides, with their sidebars on nutrition and sketches of fetal development, I reread the passages on *calculating the due date.*

Miscalculation happens easily if the woman has irregular cycles or can't remember when her last period started. Even ultrasounds, which can measure the size of a fetus, can't fully correct for this, since embryos at twelve or sixteen weeks gestation can be different sizes, just as babies at nine months gestation or six months life can be. There's not as much variation at twelve or sixteen weeks gestation is there is later on, but being off by just a day or two can make the difference as to whether, months later, a woman is considered a week postdate or still short of that mark.

THOUGH TO BE SURE, such an error was unlikely in our case. We'd done intrauterine insemination, so I'd kept close track of my periods. Calculating from the first day of my last period, the hospital had recorded my probably date of conception as January 29. So we were confident that the due date of October 30 was accurate.

THOUGH MONTHS LATER, when we went through our papers, we realized that our last insemination had been on February 4. This would have placed my due date on November 5. If my due date had been November 5, then my naturally occurring labor on November 11 would have come before I hit the one-week postdate mark. Even a hospital-based obstetrician wouldn't have recommended induction.

BUT STILL, my official due date was October 30, so the doctors would have made recommendations based on that date.

AND IN ANY CASE, though I appreciated Glenn's faith in the strength of my backbone, I wasn't entirely sure how hard I'd have pushed back.

I knew that one of the reasons I'd switched to a midwife was my fear that the doctor-patient dynamic I favored—a collaboration between a medical professional and a highly competent adult—would, by the end of the pregnancy, have given way to the dynamic of a hugely pregnant woman being managed by an expert. I'd doubted my ability to resist this dynamic in the delivery room, as I'd suspected that my training in good manners would have made it difficult for me to say "no" to medical procedures being urged on me, even if they clearly weren't necessary. And I wasn't entirely sure I'd have been able to resist this dynamic in prenatal visits toward the end of my pregnancy.

I had my answer. Basing their recommendation on an incorrect date of conception, the doctors would have recommended induction, and I might have gone along.

Or I might not have.

AND FINALLY THERE WAS THIS: In March, as the first rhubarb shoots began to pierce the earth, I was interviewed by a nurse from the Iowa Board of Nursing. The nurse-investigator, whose supremely unsensible shoes suggested relief at the fact that she now had a job that didn't require her to be on her feet all day, asked about my practitioner.

The purpose of the investigation was to determine whether Deirdre's practice fulfilled the "standard of care" established by the nursing profession. If not, the board would determine what disciplinary action was warranted. The Iowa Board of Nursing had licensed Deirdre; it had the power to revoke her license.

The allegations in the case included, "Failing to provide adequate care, including antenatal testing, to clients who had reached or surpassed forty-one-weeks gestation."

The nurse-investigator translated for me: "Did Deirde recommend an ultrasound when you went a week postdate?"

I answered, "No. She said we'd talk about it at the next visit."

The results of the investigation came twenty months after Thor's death in the form of an "informal disposition" which Deirdre requested in order to "avoid the burden, expense, delay, and uncertainties of a contested case hearing."

According to the terms of the informal disposition:

Deirdre did not admit to the allegations made against her.

The board ceased its investigation and so did not rule on the allegations.

Deirdre was required to relinquish her license for six months.

Deirdre was required to practice under supervised probation for twenty-four months upon reinstatement of her license.

I had my answer. There would be no official answer, at least regarding the question of whether Deirdre had neglected the standard of care in not referring me for an ultrasound.

But then, it hardly mattered.

Because an ultrasound wouldn't have detected anything anyway.

WHEN PEOPLE ask, "Would things have turned out differently had it not been a home birth?" I answer, "Maybe. It's hard to know for sure."

3

**PROCEDURES REGARDING TAXES, DEATH CERTIFI-
cates, autopsy reports, insurance, health spending accounts,
and free samples of infant formula following a stillbirth.**

1. Receive, a few days after the stillbirth, the thick packet
   from the insurance company regarding claims filed by the
   hospital for your emergency treatment. Just note it. You
   don't owe anything. Insurance covers it.
2. Receive, a few days after the stillbirth, the thick packet
   from the insurance company regarding claims filed by the
   hospital for its efforts to resuscitate your baby. Be alarmed.
   They will not cover those claims, because your policy does
   not list that child as your dependent.
3. Phone your insurance company. Tell the representative
   about your stillborn baby. Note that she feels obliged to
   alter her tone while you don't care. You called about an
   insurance claim. Thank the representative after she explains
   that they will make your baby your dependent for one
   month, November 2008, which will enable them to cover
   the charges.
4. When the ambulance company bills you for your baby's
   ambulance but not your own, because the insurance paid

its claim for your ambulance but rejected its claim for your baby's, call them too. They will tell you that once your insurance company has established that your baby is your dependent, they will refile your claim.

5. Receive the second thick packet from the insurance company regarding claims filed by the hospital for its efforts to resuscitate your baby and by the ambulance company for your baby's transport. Just note it. You don't owe anything.

6. Take the infant formula that arrives in the mail to the homeless shelter. Wonder when the form you filled out in the hospital to take you off mailing lists for new mothers will take effect.

7. Celebrate your older son's birthday.

8. Receive, on December 24, the autopsy report in the mail. Read its ten single-space, typed pages. Confirm that each and every one of your baby's organs, each and every one of your baby's systems, was well-developed and healthy.

9. Answer the doorbell, while you are reading the autopsy report, to let in the funeral home director, who has stopped by with your baby's death certificate. Go over it with him. Note a few errors. He will correct them and send it back.

10. Celebrate Christmas.

11. Ten weeks after the stillbirth, realize that you have not received any mail from your insurance company regarding reimbursement for your midwife's charges.

12. Contact your midwife to ask if she has filed a claim. You paid her in advance. She was to file the claim after the birth so you would be reimbursed.

13. Listen as she tells you she hasn't filed because she didn't

know how to record her efforts to resuscitate your baby. Tell her that the hospital didn't hesitate to file their claims regarding your baby. Remind yourself not to get sarcastic. Tell her your insurance company has made your baby a dependent for the month of November, and so she can file whatever charges she needs to file.

14. Open the envelope containing the insurance company's reimbursement for your midwife's charges for prenatal care, labor, and delivery. Be shocked. You understood that they would only reimburse 60 percent since your midwife is off-plan, but you thought it would be 60 percent of her charges. Instead, it will be 60 percent of their "standard and customary" reimbursement for labor and delivery. Look closely at the paperwork. You know that your midwife's charges are less than the hospital's fees for prenatal care and labor and delivery, but you also know that your insurance company has negotiated a lower reimbursement rate with the hospital. You are being reimbursed 60 percent of this lower rate.

15. Contact your insurance company to see if anything can be done. They will tell you they can only adjust a payment if the provider submits a new claim.

16. Contact your midwife to see if she can submit a new claim. Explain that you have a health spending account to cover expenses not covered by insurance, but that it doesn't have much money in it, so you must get as much covered by insurance as possible. Appreciate her assurance that she will see if there are ways she can re-do the billing so more is covered by insurance.

17. Steel yourself. It will only get worse.

18. Open the envelope containing your insurance company's response to your midwife's claim for her efforts to resuscitate your baby. Your insurance will not cover it.

19. Contact your midwife. Tell her the insurance company has rejected the claim regarding her efforts to resuscitate your baby. Listen as she promises to take it up with them.

20. Wait.

21. After two weeks, contact your midwife again. Listen as she explains that she spoke to the insurance representative on the phone. She was on hold for a long time, then passed from representative to representative. The insurance company does not have a code for resuscitation by a midwife. The insurance company will only process a reimbursement if there is a code. Wonder silently if your midwife would have let the matter drop there if you had not called. Hate yourself for wondering. Listen as your midwife promises to take it up with the insurance company again and refile the claim.

22. Explain to the woman who prepares your taxes that your baby did not get a social security number and so you cannot claim him as your dependent for 2008.

23. If it is April, which it must be because taxes are due, realize that the deadline for reimbursements for your health spending account is also approaching, and you have not received any statements from your insurance company about the claim your midwife was to file after you last spoke to her.

24. Call your midwife. Tell her the deadline is approaching. She will tell you she submitted a new claim three weeks earlier.

25. Call your insurance company. They will tell you they

received no new claim. Be alarmed that you have begun to find the insurance company more trustworthy than your midwife.

26. Call your midwife. Tell her the insurance company has received no new claim.

27. On the day before the deadline for submitting paperwork for the health spending account, submit what you have. It will arrive after the deadline, and so the benefits office will reject the claim.

28. Phone the benefits office to explain that you were waiting for the paperwork from the insurance company that should have arrived after your midwife submitted her latest claim. The benefits office will ask you for records of all your transactions and a copy of the last claim your midwife submitted, the one the insurance company did not receive. The benefits office will want to know why she submitted a claim in late January for a stillbirth that occurred in mid-November.

29. Contact your midwife. She will explain that she submitted her first claim only in late January because she had hired someone to do her billing and insurance for her, but she discovered after two months that he hadn't done a thing, and so she then had to go back and do two months' worth of claims. She has never mentioned this before. Be suspicious. Remind yourself that the fact that you are suspicious does not mean that she is lying.

30. Thank your midwife when she brings you the paperwork to deliver to the benefits office. Note that the packet includes a print-out of an email from an insurance representative admitting to being as perplexed as she is that there seems to be no code for her work, and note that it also includes a

copy of a claim dated mid-March. Wonder if she really prepared and submitted it then or whether she just did it now and back-dated it. Hate yourself for wondering. Remind her that this is just for the health spending account, but you would still like to see if your insurance company will pay more, since the health savings account won't cover the full amount remaining anyway. Ask her to re-file the claim she said she filed a few weeks ago, the one dated mid-March, which the insurance company says it never received.

31. Hear nothing more from your midwife or insurance company. Understand that the insurance company received no further claims.

32. Understand that you must let the matter drop. You cannot fight this battle. There are too many other claims on your slight reserves of emotional energy.

33. Recognize that your desire to win the battle with the insurance company is a diversion. It's not that much money. You want to win the battle with the insurance company because you lost the battle for your baby.

34. Speak with your midwife many months later. Not about the insurance, which you have let drop; speak to her about the stillbirth. You have not been ready to do this before, but now you are. You want to hear her experience of it. Sit on the front porch as you do this. It is late summer.

35. Listen to her story.

36. Be touched.

37. Be touched by her description of how the stillbirth affected her. Be moved by her dedication to her patients.

38. Be impressed as she tells you it wouldn't have happened had you been receiving hospital care, because the hospital

would have induced. The pale doctor who avoids eye contact said this to you months ago, but even if he was right, he was also self-interested. It's different when your midwife says it. Be reminded why you liked your midwife in the first place. Admire her honesty.

39. Become comfortable. Talk about things you hadn't meant to talk about.

40. Be surprised when you begin to choke up. Be surprised because it is not talking about the stillbirth that makes you cry, but talking about the insurance, which you hadn't meant to talk about, because you'd had to let it drop. Tell her you are surprised this is making you cry. Tell her that the business with the insurance feels like adding insult to injury. Tell her you have realized you must let it drop. You cannot fight this battle. There are too many other claims on your slight reserves of emotional energy.

41. Be embarrassed when your midwife offers to reimburse you for the difference between what insurance paid and what insurance should have paid. She earns much less than you do. She has worse insurance than you do. She has no health spending account.

42. Say no.

43. Listen as your midwife tells you she will take it up again with the insurance company. See how she looks you in the eye as she says that she could not prevent your injury, but she will do everything in her power to correct this insult. Nod as she asks you to get her copies of the paperwork.

44. Deliver the paperwork your midwife has requested.

45. Wait. You will not hear from her again. You will get no further notification from your insurance company that she

has submitted another claim, and that they have denied or approved the claim.

46. Wonder at the fact that you hate your midwife not because your baby died but because, as far as you can tell, she didn't take a single step with your insurance without your prodding, and once you stopped prodding, she stopped trying.

47. Recognize that you may be missing part of the story.

48. Acknowledge the irony of the fact that you are angry at her though none of this would have happened if the insurance company had paid 60 percent of her fees, which are lower than the hospital's fees to begin with, and if the insurance company had had a code for attempted resuscitation by a midwife. Recognize that the insurance company is faceless, and so there is no one to hate there, but that your midwife has a face, and so it is easy to hate her. Recognize that the paperwork required by insurance companies is a nightmare for independent practitioners while hospitals have whole staffs dedicated to filing claims. Recall that your midwife spent many hours on the phone with the insurance rep on your behalf.

49. Hate her anyway.

4

I HATED HER ANYWAY.

But I also remembered the story she told on the front porch, in the late-summer heat. I didn't remember it as conversation, as a back-and-forth between us, because my part didn't matter. What mattered was that she also had a story.

FOR A few days after it happened, she'd wake up, and for two or three seconds it would seem like a normal day.

THEN SHE would remember. Thor had died. Her head whirled and acid rose in her throat. But she had clients, appointments. Two of them the very next day. She had to act as if everything were normal.

She had been delivering babies for twenty-four years. Twenty-three years as a direct-entry midwife, this last year as a certified nurse-midwife. Never a death.

The midwives in the hospital didn't like her. It was a general hostility toward home birth, but also a special dislike of her for being so visible, so insistent, she felt sure of that. They'd never even met her! They'd never sat down in a room together, never had a conversation in which they would learn how knowledgeable and responsible she was, that she was just as serious about her job as they were about theirs. Instead, the nursing establishment had tried to shut her down. The Iowa Board of Nursing had already placed her under probation once, for having practiced earlier without a license—which she had, but only because Iowa refused to license certified professional midwives. What she'd been doing would have been perfectly legal in most states. And anyway, now she had her license.

She loved delivering babies, caring for pregnant women and new mothers. This was her calling. She loved being able to see women in their own homes, or inviting them to prenatal appointments in her own, where the cats leaped about and where she could strap the monitor onto a woman reclining on the sofa, not on a cold examining table with her legs in stirrups. She knew some women had had bad experiences with pelvic exams, or worse, with sexual abuse, and they hated being touched or prodded with implements or stared at "down there." She rarely used a speculum. She did pelvic exams the way midwives had done for centuries, with their hands, except that she used a latex glove and lubricant. She always said ahead of time, "I'm going to touch you" so there was no shock, and she maintained eye contact throughout—she looked at her patients' faces, not their genitals. She knew how to feel the hardness and angle of the cervix, and whether it was dilated.

She called her patients "clients." Maybe this downplayed her role as a medical professional. But it empowered her clients, made it clear that they were the ones making the decisions, lessened the hierarchy that so intimidated patients. They'd decided to hire her; she served at their pleasure.

She loved delivering babies in people's homes, in the aqua doula. It was beautiful. Her clients played music that soothed them. They might have their toddlers present, and those toddlers broke the tension by pretending to have labor pains themselves, scrunching up *their faces and pushing like they were about to poop, climbing into the water with their mamas. She loved catching the baby, or watching the partner catch the baby and then hand it over to the mother to hold against her breast, out of breath. She loved coaching the partner, suggesting ways to support the laboring woman. She loved watching partners' relationships develop, over the course of all those prenatal visits, during the delivery, during the post-natal visits. She knew her clients and their families in ways that hospital professionals did not.*

Sometimes a birth was tricky. She'd had to do resuscitations more than once. This is what midwives did; it was part of the job. Sometimes there was a hospital transfer. Sometimes an emergency developed, or a woman simply got too tired or hurt too much and wanted pain medication. That meant it was time for the hospital, which was fine. Some direct-entry midwives brought their laboring patients to the hospital and then disappeared, because they didn't want to get into trouble. She found that unconscionable. The hospital might need medical information that only the midwife could provide. You don't abandon a patient to save your own skin.

Hospitals were a good thing; high-tech intervention was a good thing. They saved lives. It was just that not everyone needed those things, and hospitals treated every birth as an emergency in the making. That's why there were so many unnecessary C-sections—something like one-third of all births in the US. If a woman was high risk, then of course she should have high-tech help. Those cases were not for midwives; they belonged in the hospital. And if something fishy developed along the way—if a pregnant woman suddenly developed high blood pressure, for example—then she needed to see a doctor, not a midwife, and follow the doctor's instructions.

But most women were not high risk. They were perfectly able to give birth without medication or interventions, if that's what they wanted to do. She loved making it possible for women to escape all that. But the medical establishment seemed intent on making out-of-hospital birth impossible. They fought against licensing direct-entry midwives. They scrutinized her every move, much more closely than midwives who worked in hospitals, she was sure of it.

Yet she knew what she was doing; she could do everything a hospital midwife could do, and some things they didn't do. She was a nurse, like they were. She could tell whether there was enough amniotic fluid and what the condition of the cervix was. She could listen to the baby's heartbeat. She could feel the baby and see if it was positioned correctly. She could reposition a breech baby. She could perform a nonstress test. She could order lab tests or an ultra-sound. She could do a resuscitation.

Some of her patients didn't want all these things. Some of them really were anti-technology, and even if she recommended a test, they didn't want to have it. That was their choice. She did reserve the right to stop treating someone who had risked out of midwife care: someone who went into labor before thirty-eight weeks or was still pregnant at forty-two, someone who developed pre-eclampsia, someone who turned out to have a risk factor she'd hidden, like smoking. Though in some cases, if all the medical indications were good, she might let a patient continue with her anyway. She'd once delivered a baby that was over forty-three weeks—but the fact was, the mother was healthy, the baby had a good heartbeat, there was plenty of amniotic fluid, the nonstress tests read fine. The baby was born in perfect health. She told that story to women who were approaching forty-two weeks but who were doing fine, so they wouldn't feel that after all this preparation for a home birth they now had to switch to the hospital. Guidelines were good, but they *were approximations: it was the specifics of the individual case that told you what you really needed to know. And she was determined not to get caught up in legalisms, because they were there to protect the practitioner, not the patient. Just like so many of those tests, so much of that monitoring, which was done to protect the practitioner and the hospital, not the patient. Even the American College of Obstetrics and Gynecology recommended against routine electronic fetal heart rate monitoring during labor, since it resulted in huge numbers of unnecessary interventions while preventing very few bad outcomes that would not have been caught by other means. But hospitals continued to use it, because a printout had become a necessary part of a malpractice defense. Hospitals were using a procedure which they knew resulted in unnecessary interventions, which had complications of their own, just to cover their asses in those one-in-a-thousand cases where a lawsuit developed! That was the hospital mentality.*

Then Thor died.

She had never thought it could happen. You never think it can happen, until it does.

To look at Lisa and Glenn in that hospital room! God, they had looked forward to that baby. They were numb.

And then, to go back to their house and clean up with Jeannie, the doula, just like after a normal birth. Sheets in the laundry, scrub the bathroom floor. And to see her other clients the next day, as if nothing had happened.

She did research on placental abruptions. Had she missed something, a warning sign? The risk factors for placental abruption were high blood pressure, smoking, gestational diabetes, and drug use—she knew that. Those women were high risk; they weren't eligible for midwife care anyway. But now it turned out that a sec-

ondary risk factor was advanced maternal age. She hadn't known that. Shit. Shit.

And then, the business of being postdate. You didn't risk out till you were at forty-two weeks. Hospitals might look at induction starting at forty-one weeks, but still, a pregnancy was not considered overdue until forty-two weeks: anything between thirty-eight and forty-two weeks was considered full-term, neither premature nor overdue. You just wanted to monitor the pregnancy carefully after the due date, do those nonstress tests, check the amniotic fluid. But then it turned out that for women over forty, the official recommendation is induction at forty weeks. It was only a recommendation, but still. For women over forty, rate of stillbirth climbs already after forty weeks, and very dramatically after forty-one weeks.

God damn it! How hadn't she known that? Lisa was low risk: even the hospital midwives had said she could do an out-of-hospital birth if that's what she wanted. Advanced maternal age was just a secondary risk factor, relevant only because of the inherent possibility of metabolic disorders that accompany aging. But Lisa had checked out fine for everything that mattered: diabetes, hypertension, and so on. She was fit. She'd had an easier pregnancy than a lot of women fifteen years younger. Lisa hadn't even had the slightest bit of nausea or fatigue, not that those were signs of a dangerous pregnancy, those things are just part of the package— but it was a reminder that the number describing someone's age doesn't necessarily tell you much about their physical condition. She'd had a perfect pregnancy belly, symmetrical, compact, with no stretch marks. She'd put on twenty-five pounds—twenty-five pounds of pure uterus, not a hint of weight gain anywhere else. Her blood pressure had been perfect. She had ridden her bike and done tai chi and water aerobics when she was as big as a house. She didn't smoke, didn't drink, ate great, had a terrific home situation, terrific partner, no stress. And Deirdre had been monitoring Lisa closely after her due date, a nonstress test every other day, exactly like they would have done in the hospital.

Except that at the hospital they would have induced.

But all the evidence had been there: Lisa and the baby were doing fine. This was just a baby who felt like taking its time, like some babies do. Lisa's first baby had also been post-date. Would it have made a difference if she had known the official recommendation for women over forty was induction at forty weeks? Who's to say, because she hadn't known. God damn it. Lisa and Glenn's baby was dead.

At the hospital, they would have induced. Although all the evidence had been there: Lisa and the baby were doing fine.

At the hospital, they would have induced, and Thor would have lived.

When something goes wrong in the hospital, the staff have supportive colleagues. Peers who know the devastation of that kind of loss, the feelings of powerlessness. Who can say, with the wisdom of experience, "You did your best, I know how you feel." Or who can offer guidance, professional, and humane: "You missed this sign, I would have done this differently, next time you should . . ." But she had no one to talk to, no peers. She was the only nurse-midwife doing out-of-hospital births in the whole state. When it came to processing this, she was on her own. In the meantime, she had to see her next client.

Was it her fault? Medical professionals make judgment calls all the time. Obstetricians do it, hospital-based midwives do it, and sometimes their judgment calls turn out to be wrong, and sometimes people die because of those judgment calls. No one tries to push them out of the profession; no one suggests shutting down hospitals because things sometimes go wrong.

But was any of that relevant? Lisa and Glenn had been her clients, and their baby was dead.

Should she tell new clients what had happened? Obstetricians don't tell their new patients if babies or mothers under their care have died. It's a given: if you work in a hospital, death is part of the package; it's not a personal shortcoming you have to disclose to prospective patients. But she felt: clients who come to me deserve to know. They expect a special kind of honesty, going outside the hospital system. So she began to tell them: I've delivered so-and-so many babies over so-and-so many years, and that included two deaths.

Because now there were two. Another one died, just a month after Thor. Two in a row. After twenty-four years of only good outcomes.

That mother had gone postdate too. With Lisa, she had been relaxed. The nonstress tests had been good, there had been plenty of amniotic fluid. She hadn't been worried about getting an ultrasound, which they would have ordered in the hospital but probably wouldn't have told her anything she didn't already know. When Lisa had come for her checkup at forty-one weeks and two days, she'd told her that at her next appointment—if there was a next appointment—they'd talk about maybe ordering an ultrasound. She'd known that Lisa would have no objection to an ultrasound; she'd already had a couple, while she was still seeing the hospital midwives. Lisa was fine with technology; she just wanted it used appropriately. But there was no next appointment.

With the next postdate woman, Deirdre wasn't so relaxed any

more. She'd wanted the woman to have an ultrasound at forty-one weeks. But the couple hadn't wanted one: they'd wanted to stay low tech. Deirdre hadn't known how hard to push; she'd decided to take it up again in a couple of days. By then they had a dead baby. They filed a lawsuit for wrongful death. It was thrown out of court.

A couple of months later there was a difficult birth. Severe shoulder dystocia. She performed a resuscitation, and the baby was fine. But she'd been scared to death the whole time. Was it possible to have three deaths in just a few months?

She wondered: How could she go on? Should she quit? Did she not belong in this profession after all? Could she practice if she were nervous and scared all the time? No, she decided, she couldn't quit. This was her calling.

Maybe the decision would be made for her. The Iowa Board of Nursing was investigating her. Another nurse had filed a complaint—that's how these investigations get initiated. One of the midwives at the hospital, she was sure. The board had suggested she just relinquish her license. No, she'd said, I have clients who are counting on me. In that case, there would be a hearing sometime next winter. She might lose her license. She fought back. She hired two lawyers.

If she had not had her license, she could have been charged with manslaughter.

And then, the nightmare with insurance. Paying a professional billing company a ton of money to file her insurance claims because she realized she was doing her clients a disservice by trying to do it herself. Going through the credentialing process with all the insurance companies yet again, because the billing company required that she start from scratch even though she'd already gotten credentialed as an out-of-network provider when she'd opened her own practice. Six weeks and all kinds of fees for getting set up with the billing company.

Only to have them do nothing other than send her a condolence letter when she faxed records from Thor's birth. She pressed to have the claim processed. November: they'd take care of it. December: it's in process. January: they'd look into it. And all this time Lisa was waiting, trying to at least get justice from the insurance company even if she couldn't get justice from whatever powers determined that her baby would have to die.

She called Lisa's insurance company directly, tried to submit the claim herself, asked them how to code her attempts at resuscitation. The insurance company offered no help, passed her from agent to agent. She looked up internet sources on coding and talked to obstetricians and their billers. She improvised coding and faxed the claim to the insurance company. The claim was denied. The code for newborn resuscitation only referred to resuscitations performed in hospitals. She requested clarification. The insurance company told her she should become an in-network provider and take a coding class.

She applied for in-network status. The insurance company denied her application because she didn't have a supervising physician. She hired a lawyer to appeal the decision. The State of Iowa didn't require her to have a supervising physician, why should the insurance company? She lost the appeal. The insurance company was a private firm and could require her to have a supervising physician even if the State of Iowa did not.

She paid court costs. She paid her lawyer. The insurance company reported her to the National Practitioner Data Bank as having an adverse action against her. The adverse action was having been denied privileges with the insurance company.

She had no income. Once she'd signed with the billing company, she'd been prohibited from billing clients directly. She could collect only on insurance claims processed by the billing company, but the billing company didn't process anything. They just sat there. October, November, December, January. She pulled out of the billing company in February.

She gave Lisa a statement of services and charges to submit. Lisa was a client of the insurance company. Maybe she'd get better customer service than Deirdre did. She didn't.

You just can't win with big insurance.

She changed her instructions to laboring women. No more mention of sixty-second-long contractions; they should simply call if they felt their labor was getting more intense. They should call if there was any bleeding. They should call if anything concerned them. She suggested having a doula present at an earlier stage of labor, even if it wasn't yet necessary to have the midwife there: the doula might catch signs of trouble that the woman and her partner might miss.

She became cautious. No more women over forty. Mandatory Group B strep screening. How far to go? If a postdate woman refused an ultrasound, should Deirdre tell her that she could no longer provide her care?

She revised her informed consent form to say that bad outcomes including death can occur. You always sign something like that at the hospital, something that warns you that the hospital might do its best and still things might turn out badly. Some clients read the form and then decided not to hire Deirdre. That was OK. They needed to know there were risks. A hospital was fine if they preferred it.

At every delivery, she thinks of Thor. She relives his birth, his death. She sees Lisa's and Glenn's drawn faces when she went to visit them a few days afterward, in the dark living room with the heavy scent of the lilies various well-wishers had sent. She hears their deafening silence over the next weeks, the next months. Lisa and Glenn were the ones with whom she had shared the experience, but Lisa and Glenn needed time to themselves, they did not want to talk to her right now, and who knew if they ever would.

She is haunted by the fact that she held Thor in her arms.

She is haunted by the fact that she had her mouth to his, trying to breathe life into him.

Thor is the stone in her heart.

5

I HAVE BECOME PRACTICAL AND REASONED ABOUT figuring out the reasons for Thor's death. Whether I share responsibility.

Grieving over here, analyzing my pregnancy and delivery over there.

It is comforting, to turn at least part of this into an intellectual task. And it's more effective, if I really want answers.

It requires persistence. Persistence to keep pushing, to keep seeking new information that might correct the answers I thought I had, but which might be incomplete. I can keep this up for months, and I do.

I have that persistence, because even though it may lead to an answer I don't like, it is a relief from crying, from feeling my flat belly, from noting the twelfth of each month, which we should have been celebrating.

But Glenn has not been doing this. He liked the early answers: "Thirty minutes decision-to-incision. Four minutes to brain injury, six minutes to death."

"We wouldn't have been in the hospital anyway—my contractions were mild and short."

Glenn also needed relief from feeling the weightlessness in his arms, from noting the twelfth of each month. He found his relief in teaching, in following the unfolding catastrophe in the

German department, whose chair had died just a few weeks after Thor and whose PhD program and perhaps departmental status had been targeted by the administration for elimination.

It's an intellectual task, following step-by-step the demise of your profession. Just like it's an intellectual task to investigate, step-by-step, alternative scenarios for Thor's birth.

Strangely comforting. Because at least it's better than feeling Thor's absence in our bodies, in the hours of our days.

GLENN AND I drive to Shel and Ann's farm. It's fall, several months after my appointment at the reproductive endocrinology clinic, when the pale doctor who avoided eye contact had said, "We would have induced." Several weeks after Deirdre had sat on our front porch and told me, "They would have induced."

I steer the car along the winding roads that trace the cliffs and bluffs of northeast Iowa. We are not driving the Adammobile: our mechanic has sternly warned us that it is now a car for driving around town, not for taking on longer trips. And so we'd bought a new car in the spring. This car is from our life after. Thor never rode in this car.

Glenn sits in the passenger seat and reads some of my writing: a piece on the stillbirth that I have submitted to a magazine. He gives a little gasp.

"What?" I ask.

"This part . . . that you think it wouldn't have happened if we'd planned a hospital birth."

"That's what Deirdre said, when she came by in August."

Glenn looks out the window. He hadn't been there—I'd wanted to see Deirdre alone—but I'd told him about our conversation. He says, slowly, "I think I missed that. I was still at the idea that it all happened so fast, we wouldn't have been in the hospital yet anyway, it was too early in labor."

"But remember? Deirdre said—this is what I'd been suspecting anyway, but when she said it, it kind of sealed it—if I'd been planning a hospital birth, I'd have been induced."

Glenn looks forward again, his face strained. "You must have told me, and I just blocked it out." He starts to weep. "Damn, damn."

I slow down the car, enough to divide my attention between him and whatever oncoming traffic might approach over the next ridge.

"You've been thinking about the delivery all along? What we thought at the very beginning?" My voice grows a little hard. Hardness has allowed me to let in the information that it would have gone differently in the hospital.

"No," I say flatly. "If we'd been planning a hospital birth it wouldn't have gotten that far in the first place."

Glenn wipes his eyes.

"You knew that," I say, meaning *you were supposed to know that.*"

Glenn bites his lip. "It just makes me have to think about my responsibility in all this." He leans his head back and looks at the gray fabric of the car's ceiling. "I was so focused on making sure you were comfortable. You were so tense thinking about a hospital birth, and so happy when we switched to Deirdre."

I speak emphatically. I want to stop him from going down this path. "It was absolutely what I wanted."

"It's just that—I never thought about my responsibility to

Thor, separate from wanting to help you." He turns his head away, closes his eyes, draws in a breath.

"But we *were* thinking about Thor," I say, knowing that what I was about to say wasn't really the point. "Remember when we went to visit the labor and delivery unit in the hospital? That was what sealed it. And it wasn't because of me. We figured I'd have to stand up for myself, but with you and the midwife there, and a doula, knowing what I wanted, we could fend the doctors off from doing unnecessary interventions if we needed to."

We cross the Mississippi into Wisconsin. The river is low: last year's floods have not returned. Eagles circle about, carried by the river breeze.

"But it became clear that once the baby was there," I continue, "that you and I and the doula and the midwife and all our planning would become completely irrelevant, because the baby is pediatrics' patient. They'd cut the cord right away, take it to a warming table, at the slightest suspicion of anything wrong, they could whisk it to NICU, making it hard for me to nurse, and then we wouldn't be able to get it out for days, till it surpasses its birth weight—even if it quickly becomes clear there's nothing wrong. We realized that no matter how much we work to avoid unnecessary interventions in my delivery, we'd have no control at all with what happens once the baby was there. I remember feeling totally in over my head at that point, like I could take care of myself in the hospital, do all the prep, know what I wanted—but we wouldn't be in a position to do what was best for Thor—let him start to breathe on his own, let him stay warm on my body and nurse, take care of minor problems in the least invasive way possible. It really came down to that even more than me and the birth, which we thought we could handle in the hospital if necessary."

All of this is true. But I'm also hoping to create a wall of facts, a wall of detail, to keep Glenn from asking about his responsibility in a way that puts nothing between himself and the big question. A way that involves tears.

How much more comfortable to resolve the question of responsibility through logic and leave the tears for grieving.

"I haven't thought about that visit in a long time." Glenn speaks softly toward the window. "I wish I knew if that's really what I'd been thinking about at the time. I don't know. Maybe you were more than I was. I think I was just thinking about you. I just wonder . . . where did my responsibility for Thor lie?"

I make a sharp left onto the gravel lane that leads to the farm. Another quarter mile and we're there. Apples ripening on the tree to the left, light burning on the porch to the right.

I turn off the ignition, open the door, and step out. When I reach my hand into the pocket of my jacket, I feel something. I pull it out. It's Thor's leg band from the hospital.

I'm wearing the deep red jacket Julia had brought to the hospital so I'd have something to wear home after having been brought in on a stretcher. This is the first time I've worn it since then. I pause on the porch and look at the leg band with Thor's name in purple ink, in a font that hasn't been updated since the nineteenth century. Pale brown streaks smear the white plastic. The meconium that had remained on Thor's body when he'd been brought to me.

When I'd held Thor in the hospital, he'd had heft and smell;

his skin and hair had had texture. Even as we'd taken pictures of Thor, at the hospital, at the funeral home, at home, I'd worried about looking at the pictures of him too much, worried that the visual would erase everything else.

But I'd carelessly thrown the brown tank top I'd worn during the delivery into the laundry. I hadn't thought to ask if we could bring home the hospital blanket in which they'd wrapped Thor. We'd had no choice but to bury Thor and cast off his heft and his texture. But I had erased his smell all by myself.

Now I think: perhaps the leg band, smeared with meconium, has Thor's scent. I draw it up to my nose and inhale deeply.

Nothing. It's just a piece of plastic.

6

WHAT DO I BELIEVE?

I BELIEVE Deirdre is an excellent practitioner. I believe her hundreds of successful deliveries and the intense loyalty of her clientele demonstrate that she provides an important service. I believe her practice of non-invasive birthing for low-risk pregnancies contributes to a necessary movement toward more sensitive forms of reproductive health care.

I believe that after years of successful practice, Deirdre made the wrong judgment call in not referring me to a doctor once I was a week postdate. I believe that judgment call resulted in Thor's death.

I believe the likelihood of her making the wrong judgment call was heightened by the fact that she felt under siege. I believe the warfare between the medical profession and out-of-hospital midwives made her reluctant to refer a low-risk pregnancy with no sign of trouble to a doctor. I believe that warfare made her value opportunities to demonstrate the wrongness of guidelines recommending intervention when there is no sign of trouble: to demonstrate that wrongness by carrying on and attending healthy births.

Though I believe her most fundamental reason for not

referring me to a doctor was much simpler: in her evaluation, it wasn't medically necessary.

I believe the likelihood of Deirdre's making a mistake was heightened by her professional isolation. I believe that isolation reduced the opportunity for informal, day-to-day talk with colleagues to remind her of risk factors that rarely come into play but which can be critical, like the dramatically higher incidence of stillbirth for women over forty starting at forty-one weeks' gestation.

I believe that my midwives in Berlin, practicing as a group and without feelings of defensiveness since local obstetricians collaborated with them, would have been more likely to refer me to a doctor.

I believe Deirdre has revised some of her practices as a result of Thor's death. I believe she remains professionally isolated, and that this isolation creates unnecessary risks for her clients.

I BELIEVE that studies showing roughly one hundred thousand preventable deaths every year due to infections introduced in hospitals demonstrate that unnecessary deaths occur in hospitals on a massive scale. I believe that studies showing tens or hundreds of thousands of additional preventable hospital deaths due to other factors confirm that such deaths are part of normal hospital operations.

I believe some hospitals are addressing preventable deaths. I believe others are resistant to change.

I believe that the likelihood of unnecessary death for any one patient entering the hospital system is minimal. And so I do not believe that Thor would have died had I been receiving hospital care.

I believe Thor is the statistic for unnecessary death in an out-of-hospital setting.

I believe someone else's child is the statistic for unnecessary death in a hospital setting.

I believe that a single unnecessary death during home birth prompts calls for abolition of out-of-hospital midwifery. I believe that hundreds of thousands of unnecessary deaths in hospitals prompt suggestions for voluntary reform. I believe the difference lies in the imbalance of power between hospitals and midwives, not the comparative level of risk of home birth versus hospital care.

I believe the medical system is in urgent need of reform. I believe that part of that reform must be to reward preventative and non-invasive care as bountifully as high tech, specialized care is rewarded. I believe that part of that reform must be to require that hospitals introduce procedures to dramatically reduce preventable deaths and injuries. I believe that part of that reform must be to choose protocols of treatment according to the medical evidence regarding the best interest of the patient, not anticipation of a lawsuit. I believe that part of that reform must be to integrate out-of-hospital midwives into the profession rather than marginalizing them from it.

I believe that instead of instituting reform, the medical system will continue to play, and be subject to, politics.

I believe that Thor died of politics.

I BELIEVE that Thor died in excruciating pain. His brain, deprived of oxygen, each cell suffocating, withering into itself, crumpling, collapsing, but still struggling, alerting the nerves that something was terribly wrong. The nerves suddenly plunged into burning acid, receiving the frantic message, sending that information in a useless loop back to the very brain that was under siege. The brain screaming in increasing desperation to the lungs that they should try something, anything. The lungs naively expanding, opening, to pull in relief, to pull in the cool air whose oxygen molecules it will quickly transmit to the bluish blood, re-reddening it, re-energizing it, so the blood can rush to the brain, restore it. The lungs instead getting meconium-filled amniotic fluid, choking the blood by transmitting precisely nothing, the blood by now dead but still pumped by the heart that hasn't yet learned that it is all over, the heart sending the useless blood to the brain cells now wrung dry as they complete the act of withering, crumpling, collapsing, because there is no knight on a white horse, the nerves don't send one, the lungs don't send one, the heart doesn't send one, the blood doesn't send one, Mama doesn't send one, Daddy doesn't send one, midwife doesn't send one. There is only the crush of suffocation, the realization that there is no help, the weakness too weak to despair, and then darkness.

V

Age of Anxiety

THOR'S DEATH WAS NOT REALLY EXTRAORDINARY, if you take the longer view. It wasn't so long ago that families routinely lost a child or two, or half a dozen, along the way to adulthood. Some historians think that parents didn't get so attached to their children back then because they couldn't emotionally afford to, and only with the decline in infant and childhood mortality did a culture of doting on children develop. But others have buried themselves in artifacts like diaries of grieving parents, and they think that parents always loved their children—at least, in the same proportions as they do now—and they just experienced terrible grief as a routine part of life in ways that we can no longer imagine. Before modern dental care, people also experienced skull-splitting pain due to rotting teeth as a routine part of life in ways we can no longer imagine.

When I was a kid, I knew only one family who lost a child: the Schwartzes, whose older son accidentally shot their younger son while showing a friend their father's handgun. That, my parents made clear, was a preventable death. The Schwartzes had allowed an unnecessary danger to infiltrate their home, even if they'd done so believing the gun would make them safer, and even if we mustn't allow our recognition of their mistake to overshadow our sympathy for their tragedy. In any case, the Schwartzes sorrowful story did not change the basic rule: children do not die.

But that belief must have been more tentative for my parents than we kids realized. Both of them had siblings who had died as children. How did they grow into adults so confident that children do not die?

My mother's little sister Midgie died at the age of six. She fell off a horse one Saturday and broke her arm, the bone puncturing the skin. My grandfather took her to the doctor, who put Midgie's arm in a half-cast, checked her into the hospital, and told Gramps they'd switch it out for a full cast on Monday. By Sunday she was dead of gangrene, which had festered unnoticed under the cast.

My mother doesn't recall sadness at her sister's death, though she was only a year older than Midgie. I always wondered whether she might have been sad had she not felt terror instead. This is what my mother remembers about Midgie's death: she and Midgie had identical dress-up dresses, which my grandmother had sewn by hand. Greenie dressed my mother and Midgie in their matching dresses for the funeral, and she insisted that my mother give Midgie, in her casket, a good-bye kiss. I imagine my mother at seven, leaning over the casket to see a girl almost as big as she was, with the same jutting chin, whose hair was lighter but just as curly, wearing the same dress, whose closed eyelids, Maggie knew, covered eyes of identical hazel color. She didn't want to kiss Midgie, didn't want to get closer to this dead replica of herself, and when she brushed the cheek of almost-Maggie with her lips, it was cold and waxy. Midgie was Maggie's shadow, and Midgie was dead. Maggie didn't want to be dead.

My mother doesn't recall having felt sad when Midgie died. But she also tells this story about her parents: One day when she was visiting them—they must have been in their seventies by then—her mother mentioned Midgie's name. Her father's eyes welled up with tears and he looked away, and asked her softly please not to talk about Midgie. Forty years later, and he still couldn't bear to think about her.

My father's parents, too, lost a daughter. I discovered this only when I was an adult, looking through my father's papers in his study, with its rust-colored shag rug and our house's one genuine curiosity: a built-in safe. There it was, on some German document or other: the listing of family members. Max, born 1891, married to Lisette, born 1900, and their three children: Erich, born 1927, Lilo, born 1928, with a telltale asterisk by her name, and Herbert, born 1930. I had never heard of Lilo.

My father said she had died within a couple of days of her birth. During his medical training, he had put together what had probably happened. Lilo must have been an Rh baby. Erich, he knew, was Rh positive while Oma was Rh negative, and in such cases a first pregnancy is usually successful, but during the delivery, when the baby's and mother's blood mingles, the mother builds up antibodies that attack a subsequent fetus with Rh positive blood. My father speculates that he may have Lilo's death to thank for his existence. Perhaps his parents had only planned to have two children, and if Lilo had survived, they'd have stopped there and my father—lucky him, with his Rh negative blood—would not have been born.

My father doesn't remember his parents speaking of Lilo, but then, he was separated from his parents before he turned nine, when they sent him and Erich off to England on the Kindertransport—the Children's Transport—to escape Nazi Germany. In the years before that, perhaps my grandparents had wanted to bury their memories of Lilo and hadn't even talked about her between themselves. Perhaps my grandparents had talked about her in private but hadn't wanted to burden their sons with their sorrow for their dead daughter. Perhaps they had talked openly about Lilo in my father's presence, but a phantom sister he'd never known hadn't held his interest. By the time he and his parents were reunited after the war, his parents had far bigger things to work through: memories of three years in concentration camps, trying to recreate a family when their two sons had spent eight years growing up without them. By then, Lilo might really have faded from their memories. Or maybe she was a reminder of a time so innocent it was now a foreign land, a time when premature death meant babies dying shortly after birth because they were sick.

Lilo's real name was Liselotte. In Jewish tradition, you don't name a child after a living relative. What if the Angel of Death comes to earth with an order for, let's say, Josef Zeligmann, and he takes two-year-old Josef lying in his crib instead of his sixty-eight-year-old grandfather smoking his pipe in the apartment upstairs? My grandparents must have figured that Liselotte was far enough from Lisette that the Angel of Death could keep things straight.

But when my parents named me Elizabeth—close enough to "Lisette" to honor my grandmother, but different enough to respect Jewish tradition, or so my parents thought—my grandparents were horrified. The Angel of Death could not be trusted to make such fine distinctions.

2

ALL THE NAMES OF NEW BABIES GO ON THE DRY-
erase board where departmental announcements go. Parents'
names, baby's name, date of birth, length, weight.

Thor's name is not there. We got hundreds of cards and
emails about his death. But no one has acknowledged that he
was born.

It would have looked like a sick joke if the secretaries had
written Thor's name on the dry-erase board. But still, I fanta-
size about sneaking into the office in the middle of the night
and writing in green pen: "Lisa Heineman and Glenn Ehrstine:
Thor Ehrstine Heineman, 11/12/08, 1:35 AM, 8 lb 9 oz."

My friend Jacki's mother had no birth certificate. She was
Choctaw and had been removed from her family and stuck in
an Indian school, and the authorities hadn't troubled themselves with paperwork. What does a little native girl need with
a birth certificate anyway, they'd probably figured. When Jacki
was taking care of her mother during her mother's last couple
of years, she tried to get the state of Oklahoma to produce a
birth certificate so she could have an easier time with various
state bureaucracies, but she had no luck. Now Jacki's mother,
like Thor, has a death certificate but no birth certificate.

THERE IS a legislative drive underway to require that states issue birth certificates for stillborn babies. A bereaved mother started it, but now anti-abortion advocates are pushing for it. If it passes, the state would be issuing birth certificates for babies who hadn't made it to their third trimester and could still legally be aborted.

Thanks a lot, anti-choicers, for making it dangerous to express grief.

3

I JOINED FACEBOOK SO I COULD SHARE BABY PIC-
tures. My first profile pictures were of me hugely pregnant.
Here with an enormous praying mantis climbing up my black
sweater. Here with me posed in profile, bare belly forward,
head turned to the camera, right hand pointing a silver trout
at the fridge, like something from Dada. Here with my shirt
pulled up and FREE THOR penned on my belly with a red
magic marker.

When I went into labor, I was flipping between Facebook
and old *Daily Show* episodes. I posted a status update. "Lisa is
in labor! Stay tooned!"

And so my sister knew to text Glenn the next morning to
find out how it had gone. And so my mother knew to call the
next morning to find out how it had gone.

My mother expected Glenn to pick up the phone, but I
did. She was surprised—she figured I'd be napping or nursing
or something. But there was no need. The baby was dead.

Glenn felt he should answer Sue's texts, but I told him:
no need, I can tell her myself, I'm not nursing or napping. I
phoned and told her: the baby is dead.

I didn't want to discuss my stillbirth on Facebook. But there
it was, my last status update. "Lisa is in labor! Stay tooned!"

I needed a new status update. "Lisa is sad. Little Thor is dead."

For the next many months, my profile pictures were of Thor's absence.

A shadow of my pregnant profile on the grass. The bird-feeder by Thor's grave—not the grave itself, just the birdfeeder, so unwitting friends wouldn't be confronted by a picture of a baby's tombstone. A dragonfly, because I had painted dragonflies on Thor's temporary grave marker and had come to imagine dragonflies as Thor's favorite insect, or perhaps as Thor himself.

Now I check Facebook and this is what I see. Jen's daughter asleep in her car seat, wearing her unicorn costume. Timothy's son on his potty with a book on his lap and the caption "The apple falls close to the tree." Cindy's baby daughter in New York, in California. Videos of Lulu running through the park.

Because that is what you do. You post pictures of your kids on Facebook.

Eventually I had to adjust my settings so I wouldn't see the updates of friends who always posted new pictures of their babies.

4

ALWAYS WITH THE BABIES.

Always the ultrasounds, which you excitedly pass around the office.

Always the announcements of births, name-weight-length-birth date, on the office dry-erase board.

Always the requests to write my state senator about the midwifery bill coming up for a hearing.

Always the strollers, lined up like an obstacle course, at the playground separating the gym from the café.

Always the forwarded magazine articles about attacks on women who breastfeed in public.

Always the Christmas letters with the photo of the happy family, the news of first steps, first words, first time at the beach.

Always the stretched-out bellies, protruding over the counter at the cash register at the co-op.

ALWAYS WITHOUT the babies.

Always the invitation to go out to dinner—always "I'll hire a babysitter, we'll go out" rather than accept our offer to bring dinner so we can eat at your place, with your baby, whom we long to see.

Always the wall of words—about your latest recording session, your plans for the summer, your in-laws' visit—demanding that I look at you, answer you: insuring that I not look down at your baby cooing in her stroller or reach down to finger her chin.

Always the sadness, the sadness that you can't invite us to come by and bring our baby, to play with your kids, you'd so looked forward to that, as if you can't invite us over without a baby.

Always the embarrassment—no, no, you couldn't possibly come by to grill in our backyard, you'd have to bring the kids and that would be boring for us—although we plead with you to let us see your kids, we adore them.

IN EARLY modern times, if something bad happened to a baby—she went missing, mysteriously fell ill, died—eyes turned to the woman who had earlier lost a baby. Her grief must be so great and her jealousy so acute that she must wish ill on other babies, or perhaps wish to snatch one for her own.

Babies everywhere, but we are forbidden to come near them.

5

I LIE IN BED WITH GLENN. I'M ON THE RIGHT SIDE, and he's on the left.

When I was pregnant, I slept on the left. I lay on my left side, slim airplane pillow under my belly, larger pillow between my legs, and Glenn held me from behind, sleeping on his left side as well, his better side, since he snores more when he sleeps on his right.

I switched to the right side when we had Thor home for the night. The co-sleeper had fit only on that side of the bed, and I'd wanted to be next to him, and so Glenn and I had switched sides, and I'd slept on my right so I could see Thor and lay my hand on his belly. Glenn had to turn his back to me so he wouldn't snore, but that was all right, we couldn't have everything, and Thor would only be with us one or two nights.

Now Thor is buried but I still lie on the right side. And on this night, winter solstice, we can hear, through the old iron grate on the bedroom floor, Adam's birthday party downstairs. He is seventeen.

The kids—they're so alive. Talking, laughing, shouting from one room to another.

Earlier, Glenn and I sat in my study while the kids partied in the kitchen, the dining room, the living room. So silly, they were; so loud. One girl blanched with embarrassment as she walked through the kitchen and realized how close we were—the study adjoins the kitchen—and hurried back to the dining room to warn the others, who had been talking loudly about sex: "You guys! Shh! Be quiet! Adam's step-" she stammered, at a loss for the right word—"Adam's step-whatever-he-is is right in the next room! He can hear everything we're saying!"

Adam's step-whatever. Glenn and I aren't married. Julia and I had been together seventeen years and raised a child for thirteen and never been married, so marrying Glenn never seemed all that necessary.

I looked at Glenn in the quiet study and raised my eyebrows.

He was smiling. "I'll take that as a sign of belonging," he said, genuinely pleased.

They were so alive, Adam and his friends. Their silliness, their rowdiness, their stumbling over what to call Glenn.

Well, let's keep it that way, I thought, so alive. I headed into the kitchen and busied myself cleaning till Adam walked through. I nodded him over. "Um, are these people planning to drive themselves home?" I asked. "Is anyone here fit to drive?"

Adam laughed. "It's fine," he said. "They'll probably just fall asleep here and drive home later. And Sue just had like one drink, early on—she can drive people home."

Like one drink? I thought.

Still, it was Sue, azure-haired Sue, Adam's best friend. She's often the designated driver. And she's often the host, when her dad is out of town, and then all the kids just sleep over at her place—a giant teenage slumber party that involves no one getting into a car.

"OK," I said. "Make sure they just sleep here if they need to. The roads are icy. I don't want any accidents."

"Yep!" Adam waved and ducked back into the dining room.

I walked back into the study, paused in the doorway, looked at Glenn, sitting on the sofa with a book. He looked up, eyes reaching like a hand to touch my cheek.

"They're so alive," I said.

I was suddenly exhausted. "Can we go upstairs and read in bed?" I asked.

"Sure. Do you think they're OK down here?" Glenn gestured with his chin toward the rest of the house.

"They're fine," I said.

Now we lie in bed, I on the right, Glenn on the left, and we hear the muffled sounds of the party downstairs. For the first time since Adam's first birthday, I relive his birth. Labor on the fifth-floor walk-up apartment in Berlin, the mad taxi ride through half the city at two on a Sunday morning, the pitch-black streets, the climb up the steps at the midwifery center, Julia holding me from behind as I perched on the edge of the bed and pushed, the midwife showing Julia how to wash the baby as I lay back on the bed, our postbirth nap as a threesome. I see in my mind our first family photo, taken by the midwife when she saw us lying there asleep.

Suddenly I jolt upright. "Glenn, right now, we have to switch places!" My heart thumps in my throat, my hands flail. I crawl over Glenn, who looks up, startled. "We have to switch places! Now!" I'm on his other side by the time I finish the sentence, and I pant and push him with my hands against his side, his hip—push him to the right side of the bed. "I have to be over here," I murmur, and pull the cover over my head, facing away from Glenn, away from the right side, curling my knees to my chest.

Glenn straightens the cover over me, silently, slowly. He picks up his book, and mine, both of which had fallen onto the bed during my flight. He lays them gently on the headboard, turns off the light, slips under the covers, now on the right side of the bed, and spoons me from behind, curling his fingers into mine, pressing his face into my hair.

The right side of the bed was where I'd lain as I'd delivered Thor.

6

IN MIDWINTER, AS I WALK HOME FROM WATER AERO-
bics, my first time since the evening I went into labor, I feel it.
My pregnant belly is back.

I used to feel it most during these walks home, as I moved
from the weightlessness of the water to the work of hauling it
through the city. Now the pregnant belly is there again.

Ghostbelly.

The ghost of an amputated limb hurts. My ghostbelly is
solid, reassuring. I feel the interior boundary between abdo-
men and uterus. Not the outside boundary where skin touches
clothing, but the inside boundary, where the belly that is me
used to segue into the larger belly, the belly that had been
Thor's. Right beyond the boundary is Thor. He is not the dead
Thor; he is the Thor who has not yet been born.

There is a light, icy rain outside, just like there had been
during my last walk home before I went into labor. That had
been a peaceful, exuberant walk. I'd been nimble, my chiropractor had freed my hips the day before, and aquacize had
loosened them yet again. Glenn had waited at home, where we
would eat the salad he'd prepared. The air had been cool, and
I had walked tall, straight, with Thor inside me and my legs
swinging free.

Suddenly the ghostbelly dissolves. Its invisible particles

scatter into the air and vanish without a sound, without the slightest tug at the inner belly that remains.

Stomach and bladder and kidney wonder at the silence next door. The eerie stillness of an apartment vacated swiftly and stealthily overnight. The neighbors you had liked, whose music and laughter you had heard through the common wall, gone all at once, leaving no note, no phone number, no forwarding address, no explanation.

But the ghostbelly returns periodically. Fifteen months after Thor's death, my body's memory is still in the water. I do not recall my pregnant belly while pouring cereal at the kitchen counter, or while climbing into the car, or while making love. But I recall it while standing naked in the locker room after aquacize. I see the towel spreading across my huge belly as I dry myself, and I feel my fingers rubbing lotion into the taut skin. As I stand under the shower and rinse the chlorine from my body, I squeeze residual drops of milk from my nipples, and I watch the water from the showerhead dilute them into invisibility before washing them down the drain.

7

LATE THAT WINTER—THOR HAD BEEN DEAD THREE months or so—Adam discovered Glenn holding me in the kitchen. I was crying, and Adam was surprised.

"I cry every day," I told him.

"Really, you do?" he asked. Teenaged Adam usually saved eye contact for easy situations, like joking around. But now he looked straight at me, his face completely unguarded. His long hair bobbed around his chin, and his soul patch and black, plastic-framed glasses gave his face dark definition. He was wearing one of the horizontally striped, long-sleeved T-shirts that made him look like a mime when he pulled his hair back into a ponytail.

"Yes, I do. That's just how it's going to be for a while."

"Wow, I had no idea," he said. He thought a minute. "I guess I just haven't had that kind of thing happen to me."

But he had gathered his own experiences of death.

WHEN ADAM was six, Maus #1 died.

We had bought two white mice—Maus #1 and Maus #2— just a couple of days earlier. They lived in a glass-walled tank on a board that rested on the steam radiator in Adam's room in Toledo, where we lived before moving to Iowa City. In the tank were a couple inches of wood chips, an exercise wheel, a little, blue ceramic bowl for food, and a water bottle, which hung upside down and let out drips through a metal tube with a ball in the end. The weight of the water pressed the ball to make a seal at the end of the tube, but even a tiny mouse tongue could push the ball to let out a drop of water. We weighted down the top of the cage with a fat book so our cat wouldn't get any ideas about knocking off the lid and fetching herself a mouse to play with.

Adam loved Maus #1 and Maus #2. Probably, he loved Maus #1 to death. Poor Maus #1 and Maus #2 needed to get adjusted to their new home, but Adam couldn't resist taking them out to play. He let the mice crawl up his arm, to his neck, into his shirt, and he'd shriek with giggles. He let the mice explore his room, which usually ended with his calling Julia or me to coax them out from under the bed or the radiator.

After dinner one evening, I discovered Maus #1 lying still on her side in the tank. I returned to the kitchen and signaled to Julia that she should come and take a look. I lifted Maus #1 out of the cage to be sure. She was dead. Her fur was so soft it was nearly liquid. I lay her back down on the wood chips.

We called Adam to the room. I said, "Adam, we have very sad news. Mommy Julie and I just came in to check on the mice, and do you know what we discovered?"

Adam shook his head, unable to fathom what could be so sad, but alarmed just the same. His mothers looked so serious.

"It looks like Maus #1 died. Do you see her lying there?"

Adam pressed his nose to the glass. Maus #1 did not look like she was sleeping. She curled up when she slept, and now she was just lying on her side, legs poking straight out.

"Should we take her out?" Julia asked.

Adam nodded, eyes welling up with tears.

I took the mouse out and laid her flat in my palm. "Here," I said. "You can pet her."

Adam reached out a finger to pet her, and his silent tears turned to sobs, and then to a wail.

"Why did she die?" he cried.

"I don't know," I said, kneeling down to his level. "When mice have a new home, there are so many new things for them to get used to, sometimes it's just too much for them, and they can't make the adjustment."

He reached out to take Maus #1, his shoulders hunched up a little, hiccupping in an unsuccessful effort to contain his crying enough to keep his hands steady.

"We'll have to bury Maus #1 outside," I said. "We'll bury her right next to the house. Do you want to write a letter for her to take with her?"

Adam nodded and pet Maus #1. He turned and carried her slowly to his low wooden table, with two kid-sized chairs, which sat beneath a window looking out at the garage. This is where Adam drew.

Adam set Maus #1 down on the table and took a piece of paper.

"Should we stay here while you write, Adam, or do you want to do it by yourself?" Julia asked.

"I'll do it by myself," he said, sniffling and looking down.

"OK." We kissed him on top of his head and left the room, and heard his crying from the kitchen as we cleaned up the dinner dishes.

Before burying Maus #1, I thought about surreptitiously copying the letter. I decided it would be dishonest: the letter was supposed to go, as Maus #1 would go. But years later, when I looked through the huge portfolio into which we stuffed Adam's art and writing from first grade, I found a story he must have written after Maus #2 died. The text read: "The. DED. MOU. S. NOW. 2 . MiS . HAVE . DiD."

The Dead Mouse. Now 2 mice have died.

By the looks of the writing it probably happened early in the fall; Maus #2 must have survived several months. The drawings show a dead mouse lying stiffly on its side; then a pile of mouse bones and mouse internal organs; then a live mouse standing on its hind legs, tail high in the air, leaning with its front paws and looking longingly into the glass bowl where the dead mouse lies; then the live mouse lying on its stomach, eyes wide open, staring forlornly ahead.

I believe Adam thought Maus #2 died of a broken heart.

Later, I planted mint in the strip of grass where Maus #1 and Maus #2 were buried, and later yet we buried our cat there. But Adam didn't cry when the cat, or subsequent pets, died. He had learned that pets can die, and the next day you can do all the fun things you'd done the day before, and laugh and be happy—that's how it turned out the day after Maus #1 died. Life had been good without Maus #1, even if it had been still better with her.

Things got more serious in high school, when kids started dying. The new boy from Chicago, Sammy, who sat next to Adam in ninth-grade English class—rumor had it, from an accidental drug overdose. No one knew for sure, because no one from the school said anything about it to the kids. Perhaps they didn't say anything because the parents hadn't wanted them to, but Adam was a ball of anger, furious that Sammy could be there one day, dead the next, and after a loudspeaker-induced moment of silence, the kids were supposed to go on with their day, do their math, their English, as if nothing had happened.

And then, the suicide: Theo, best friend of Ted, who was one of Adam's closest friends. He shot himself when Adam was in tenth grade. Afterward Adam watched as Ted, an actor and musician and always a sensitive kid anyway, fell apart, disappearing from school for a couple of weeks, then frantically trying to make all his friends happy while slipping into utter confusion about what his own life was supposed to be all about.

Late in the summer when I was pregnant with Thor, Adam began work on an animation about a boy who attempted suicide. The narrator had to finish the job when he discovered his friend mortally wounded from his self-inflicted shot, but not yet dead and suffering terribly. Adam worked on the storyboard for weeks, finishing not long after Thor died. He showed me the storyboard, and I was touched, because usually he kept his work secret till he was done. But the story was so dark, and the night outside the kitchen window was so dark, and my new life with a dead baby was so dark, that I had to turn the pages quickly, missing the chance to linger over Adam's art, which I usually consumed hungrily. Over the next months, as I wrote about Thor, Adam worked on his animation about a boy whose friend committed suicide.

Adam, too, had settled into life with a dead baby. In the hospital, when Adam had let the words slip from his mouth, "It doesn't really mean that much to me," and then been embarrassed, I'd told him not to worry what other people thought he should be feeling, he should have his own experience of this. And then I'd been embarrassed too, because I'd thought I sounded like a pop-psychology book. But I repeated those words, or words like them, a lot more over the next weeks, because I'd been right. When Adam went to school that day and told people what had happened, they wanted to cry with him, and when he explained that it was OK, people found that more distressing than if Adam had been distressed. People he barely knew offered condolences and hugs at the memorial service, and he didn't want to be rude, but he really didn't need them. He was a good sport though: he did whatever he knew would be meaningful to Glenn and me. He painted the lid of Thor's casket. He held the end of one of the straps that let the casket down into the grave.

THOR'S DEATH hadn't meant that much to Adam. And so he was surprised when he learned that three months later, I still cried every day.

"Wow, I had no idea," he said. He thought a minute. "I guess I just haven't had that experience, like you have, and Ted."

"That's OK," I said. "It's not much fun anyway."

"The thing is, I can't really think of anyone dying where it would affect me like that. I mean, even with Theo—he was a friend, but it just didn't hit me."

"I don't think you can predict when it will."

"I just can't imagine whose death would be like that for me," he said. And then, softly, "Except for my mothers, if one of them died. That would be bad."

He understood. "Yes," I said. "That would be bad."

8

EVEN AFTER WE'D BURIED THOR, GLENN AND I STILL needed to be his parents. Thor was two weeks old, then three weeks, then a month, and we had to care for him. That's what you do for your new baby. And so we found projects.

I went to the paint-your-own-pottery shop and made a temporary grave marker, which I decorated with light blue dragonflies and pounded into Thor's grave before the deep freeze came. I drove with my friend Michaela to a photographer in the countryside who made a life-sized print of my photo of Thor's casket lid. I had it framed and gave it to Glenn for Christmas. Glenn made a careful list of everyone who had sent flowers or brought food, who had come to the memorial service or written a card or donated a tree. I set a photo of Adam's painted casket lid against a deep blue background and had two hundred prints made. At the office supply store I ordered a rubber stamp that identified the picture: "Adam Heineman, Thor's Casket, 2008. Acrylic on pine." Together, Glenn and I glued the photos to blank cards, stamped the backs of the cards, and wrote thank-you notes to everyone on Glenn's list, over a hundred people.

And we visited Thor's grave almost daily: the cemetery was only three blocks from our house. We installed a birdfeeder, brought sheaves of wheat from Shel and Ann's farm, erected a homemade wreath. We told Thor what we'd had for breakfast, which friends we'd seen, what Adam was up to. We brought pinecones and odd-shaped rocks, and we filled his birdfeeder with sunflower seeds. With each fresh snowfall Glenn stamped the words "HI THOR" in six-foot-high letters next to his grave. At night we looked up at the sky and told Thor of the thousands of stars.

Spring semester began and Glenn and I went back to teaching, but visiting Thor, talking about Thor, parenting Thor remained the real content of our days. Israeli troops invaded the Gaza Strip. Obama was inaugurated as president. The Icelandic banking system collapsed. We visited Thor, refilled the birdfeeder, stamped "HI THOR" into the snow.

In mid-April Glenn called Phil Michel, the manager of Memorials by Michel. Phil had promised to let us know when they would erect Thor's headstone so we could be there. But he'd forgotten to phone. It turned out that Thor's headstone was ready, and the ground had started to dry out after the spring thaw. They would install the base the next day.

I was edgy that Friday morning. I wanted to arrive early to remove everything that had accumulated at Thor's grave: the temporary marker; the shepherd's crook with its sheaf of wheat and the birdfeeder heavy with black sunflower seeds; the eucalyptus pods, beach stones, redwood bark, and pinecones from our trip to California in January; Michaela's pink, broken-heart stone from her meditation retreat in Bavaria. I was afraid the workers wouldn't recognize that the stones and pieces of bark were intentional, and they'd just dump them aside; and anyway, I wanted Glenn and me to remove even the big obvious items ourselves.

It was sunny, and although it was still cold enough that we wore our winter coats, it was warm enough that we didn't have to huddle in them. If you looked closely, you could see buds on the trees: in a couple of weeks they'd start to leaf out. As we rounded a curve at the top of one of the gentle hills in the cemetery, we saw the Memorials by Michel truck down the hill and to our right. This was a different section of the graveyard from Thor's, but we knew that after the winter there was a long backlog of stones to be put in. We walked on to Thor's spot to sit with our temporary decorations one last time, and to wait.

It turned out they'd been there the day before to unbury the metal pins that marked the corners of each gravesite and to label the spot where the workers were to install the headstone. There was an orange spray-painted arrow to show the workers where to dig, like the red "X" that surgeons use to make sure they amputate the correct leg. The arrow was on the site to the left of Thor's.

Glenn and I looked at each other. What now? Had we put the temporary marker on the wrong spot? No, we were sure we hadn't. When we'd started making our pilgrimages there, the rectangular cut in the ground from the burial had still been plain to see: rough, hacked edges, with patches of grass resting at cockeyed angles where the graveyard workers had filled in the hole above Thor's casket. Or had we lost track in those weeks after the snow had fallen but before we'd gotten the temporary marker in? At the time, we'd jammed a stick into the ground to mark the spot. Had the stick somehow migrated? Perhaps it had fallen over and someone had tried to put it back up, but in the wrong spot?

My stomach grew tight. I thought of coming all winter

long, talking to Thor, checking in on the birds, bringing little rocks and pinecones, all, absurdly, on a chunk of dirt where no one was buried—and Thor lying in the next grave over, indifferent to our mistake. His weight below the ground on the left, ours above ground to the right, out of synch, unbalanced.

Glenn said he knew what had happened: they'd put in Thor's casket crooked. He remembered having had this sense way back when we'd visited the grave before the snow had covered it. The cuts in the ground didn't lie straight, he'd thought at the time. Didn't I remember how he'd tried to line the temporary marker up with the head of the casket, and I'd kept telling him it was at an angle, it should face more to the left, because that's where the foot of the plot was? That was because the casket wasn't lined up right, he said.

"I remember," I told him, wondering at Glenn's ability to come up with roundabout and unlikely ideas rather than follow the rule that I followed religiously: the simplest explanation is usually the best.

I spoke again: "So what kind of bureaucratic mind do you suppose is at work here? To come with a bottle of spray paint and orders to mark site 393 for Thor Ehrstine Heineman, and dutifully paint an arrow on site 393, when this is what you see." I gestured at the two sites.

"I know," Glenn said. "Undisturbed grass at 393, and right next to it 394 overflowing with decorations. Including a marker with the name 'Thor Ehrstine Heineman.'"

The truck drove up and two men got out, both wearing sweatshirts and dark glasses against the bright sun. They walked down the hill, toward Thor's grave, where we waited. I pointed from the orange arrow to Thor's cluttered grave and shouted, cheerfully to let them know I was sure it was just some silly mistake we'd all laugh about, "I think you have the wrong spot!"

Before they had a chance to orient themselves, Glenn started somberly: "I think the problem is that the casket is angled." He drew a line on the ground with his foot to show where he thought the edge of the casket was. He described in greater detail what he thought had happened; how the cut in the earth might in fact have crossed just a bit into the next plot over, which they had marked; how he had thought it was crooked from the beginning. I grew irritated.

I didn't buy Glenn's crooked-plot theory. And even if it was true, I didn't see that it mattered. What if the casket *was* a little crooked? The problem, it was dawning on me, was that we'd decorated the right spot all along. This was where Thor was buried. But they'd put him in the wrong place. He was supposed to be in that spot with the orange arrow. The cemetery workers had marked that spot because that's where the records said he was, and the records said he was there because that's where we'd asked to have him buried.

The Michel's workers went to get someone from the cemetery management. I paced anxiously, kicking the ground. This was all wrong. Probably the management and Glenn would figure it was OK if we just switched spots, since we'd also bought 394. But 394 was at the end of the row. Thor was supposed to go into 393, one spot in. Either Glenn or I might be cremated and go into 393 with him, and the other would go into 394, or perhaps we'd both be cremated and go into 394, and we didn't know how Adam might fit into this—we had space for him if he wanted it, but maybe he'd grow up and settle somewhere else and want to be buried there—but the point was that Glenn or I or both of us would cradle Thor from the outside, shield him from the edge. The spot at the end of the row was too exposed for a little baby.

Glenn continued on about the angle. He worried that when it came to burying us in 393 someone would discover that it already had some remains in it and there would be problems. There it was—proof that he thought it didn't matter if Thor was in the last plot in the row.

"By the time we're buried," I said, "there will be nothing left of Thor or his casket."

"Maybe some bones," Glenn said.

He seemed to be missing the point. Thor wasn't supposed to be at the end of the row. Thor was supposed to be one spot in. He was in the wrong place, the wrong place, the wrong place. He was perched precariously on the edge, like a baby in danger of rolling off the bed, and the best we'd be able to do would be to try to hold onto him from behind, from the safe spot that was supposed to have been his.

Rick, the cemetery manager, drove up in his golf cart, the workers from Michel's following in their truck. I called brightly, in a panicky attempt to keep the situation light, "Hey, you buried our kid in the wrong place!"

Glenn stood behind Thor's temporary marker and started: "Our main concern . . ."

I growled. Glenn looked at me and revised his language. "*My* concern is that when Thor was buried, it was at an angle"—he gestured with his foot to show the alleged angle—"and I believe the lower portion of his casket might actually cross over into the next plot."

I interrupted, stamping my foot like a little kid, "I'd just like to go on record as saying that the problem is that Thor is buried in the *wrong place*, who cares about some angle, and what are we supposed to do about the fact that he's not where he's supposed to be?"

Four pairs of eyes swiveled toward me. But I was done. I had no more to say. Were they expecting me to propose a solution to this problem?

Rick said they'd do whatever we wanted. They could move Thor's remains to 393. They could switch the names on the deeds to show that Thor was in 394 and that we also owned 393, which was empty. I noted with some satisfaction that Rick didn't even take up the supposed problem of Thor's poking a toe from 394 over to 393. Glenn looked at me. He'd realized from my outburst that I was upset, and he did what he always does in such circumstances: he dropped whatever was worrying him to tend to me.

What do you want to do, he asked with his eyes.

The Michel's guys said we could postpone the whole thing if we needed more time. They could come back another day. I told them we needed a few minutes to talk about it. They went away to investigate another plot on their list for that morning.

I sat down on the ground, facing the temporary marker. Glenn sat down next to me.

"We can sleep on it," he said, looking softly at me.

"I don't want them to disturb Thor." My voice cracked as I stared ahead at the temporary marker.

"OK," Glenn said. "We'll have them leave it as it is."

I tensed at the suggestion of resolution. "No," I said. "We should sleep on it." I looked at my fists. "I don't know what to do." I turned my head away from Glenn's. "I don't want him on the edge. I need to think about it."

Glenn got up and walked around. He picked up some stones on the far side of the temporary marker and turned them over in his hand. He walked behind me and looked at the two sites next to each other.

I looked at the stones and eucalyptus pods and pinecones in front of the dragonfly marker. I had never seen them from this angle, right at ground level. It had always been too snowy or wet to sit. At least down here I was away from all those men. Workmen with sweatshirts and shovels. Glenn with professorial beard. Rick with clipboard. Just leave me alone with my baby.

I sure as hell didn't want to move Thor. He was where he was, lying perfectly peacefully. It wasn't his fault the cemetery people had screwed up. Why should he be disturbed? Right now, he was still lying in his casket as we'd left him—skull above vertebrae, backbone extending straight, arms protruding from shoulders, legs from hips with knees drawn up in that baby-froggy way. The movement would surely cause the pine casket, now sodden with snow melt, to disintegrate. Thor's partially decomposed body would fall to bits; his bones wouldn't make any sense anymore. Then we'd put up a gravestone in a place where he hadn't even been buried. Because he'd been buried in November, in the last spot on the row. No reburial would change that. A reburial would just be moving a bunch of bones.

But, but . . . I looked toward Thor. I realized then that I'd always looked at his spot from the same angle: the angle I'd be facing if I lay in the last spot with Thor one spot in, the way it was supposed to be. My body felt a little heavier on the right side—I'd always imagined lying on my right side with my back to the edge of the row, so I could face Thor and cradle him from his left, as I had on those nights when we'd brought him home for overnight stays. I tried to change my orientation. I shifted to the other edge of Thor's grave and tried to put my weight on my left, so I'd cradle him from that side. It didn't work. My right arm, leg, hip were still heavier. I looked over Thor at the ravine from this side. It looked all wrong—weedy, interrupted by the access road, no logic to the curve that descended to the stream bed.

It occurred to me that this was the view I would have inflicted on Thor if he'd been where he was supposed to be, facing me, as I faced him and the nicer view. It also occurred to me that I should be able to convince my body that lying on its left felt right. Perhaps it would be nice for Thor to have us to one side and the open woods to the other. Thor had never known anyone but me and Glenn. But he did know the birds and squirrels and deer who visited from the forest. Maybe he'd like to have us on one side and the woods on the other, rather than us on one side and strange people on the other. Glenn sat down next to me again.

"Let's tell them to just put up the stone," I said. "I don't want to disturb Thor."

The guys from Michel's installed the base and told us they'd be back at nine the next day to finish up, after the base had had a chance to dry. By 8:15 the next morning I was nervous and so we headed to the cemetery, walking slowly, since it was only ten minutes from our house. A flock of crows drifted from one tree to the next, thousands of wings making the deep, rippling sound of heavy paper. They settled for a short while, then moved with aloof synchronicity to the next tree for reasons known only to them. Hundreds more crows approached lazily from the northwest, and their occasional caws opened a hole in the dull, gray sky. As we emerged from the cedar-lined walkway that opens onto Thor's section of the cemetery, Glenn said, "I think they're already there." He squinted. "I think they've already done it. They're finishing up." It was 8:50.

I walked fast and furious toward them, leaving Glenn to decide if he wanted to keep up. Twenty feet away, I said to them, loudly, through gritted teeth, "YOU'RE EARLY." They froze, looked up at me, looked at each other. I stood with clenched fists. "We wanted to be here when you put it up. Phil told us nine o'clock. When did you get here? When did you start working?" I stared at them.

"Um, we got started at 8:30. That's the time Phil told us," one of the men said carefully.

"We tried to call you," another said, "but you didn't answer. We left a message."

"Of course we didn't answer," I spat back. "We were on our way here."

"We can take it back down," said a third man, one of two new ones who hadn't been there the day before. "We just put it up. It hasn't set yet. Then you could watch us do it."

"Yeah, that would be good," I said, offering no apology for the extra work. Glenn had just caught up to me.

The last two days had probably reminded the workers of why they preferred to install gravestones without the families present. They rushed to take the stone off and set it on two wooden planks to the side. One of the men scraped the sealant off the base; another went for a bottle of windex and a rag to polish it. Glenn and I kneeled by the base, touched the impossibly smooth polished granite with our hands.

We stepped back and nodded to the men: they could reassemble it now. One squirted some gray sealant; the biggest one picked up the stone and set it in place. (How much did it weigh, I asked. A hundred forty pounds, he answered.) Another used a ruler to make sure it was centered, then two of them pressed down on the top of the headstone, hard, to make the seal. They wiped the extra sealant away, polished it again with windex, and were done. We thanked them. They left.

Glenn and I sat down cross-legged on Thor's grave and looked at the stone. I was exhausted from the last two days. Now it was time for peace to descend.

But it didn't. I'd loved our homemade decorations, which fluttered in the wind and leaned unevenly in the mud. Now I looked at a rigid stone, carved by someone else, which would hurt you rather than give way if you bumped into it.

Glenn got up and walked around to see the stone from different angles, and then from behind. He crouched down and beckoned me over. A little metal tag reading "Designed by Memorials by Michel, Solon, IA" was wedged between the stone and the base. The sealant wasn't hard yet, so we pulled it out. We didn't want Thor's gravestone to be advertising space. Besides, we had designed the stone, with its dragonflies at the top left and right corners and the simple text in a gentle, curved font: "Thor Ehrstine Heineman. Nov. 12, 2008." Memorials by Michel had carved and installed it.

We came back later that day to redecorate. We put the birdfeeder and the rocks and shells and other little things back in their places, and we planted some daffodils that I'd dug up from our garden.

As we walked away, Glenn said, carefully, "You know, I think it's fine where Thor is, and we did the right thing in leaving him there."

"I think so too," I said.

"And I like the stone," he continued.

I paused. "I like how small it is." We'd ordered a stone much smaller than anything else in Michel's shop. It seemed fitting for a baby.

"But . . . I'm still bothered by the fact that he's in there angled."

I took a breath and tried hard to hold onto my fragile equilibrium. "I really don't think there's going to be a problem with burying us in the next one over."

"No, I don't mean that," Glenn said. "It's just . . ." His voice broke a little. "It's just . . . when I come to visit him, I want to know where he is."

I stopped in my tracks and looked at him. He'd been harboring that anxiety all along. I'd been of no help.

"Next time we're there," I said, taking his hand, "show me where you think the perimeter of the casket is. We'll plant some low-rising flower to mark it. Something that blooms in spring before mowing season starts."

"Yes," Glenn said hopefully. "Yes. That would be good."

I pointed to the scilla that grew wild in the part of the cemetery we were now walking through. "Something like that," I said. The tiny purplish-blue blooms bobbed delicately in the breeze; the narrow leaves grew upright, only their dark green color distinguishing them from the surrounding grass.

Glenn's eyes welled up with relief. "They're pretty. I like them. Yes. A rectangle to mark where he is."

He stooped to investigate the graves on which the flowers grew. "Look at the headstones," he said. They belonged to three children from a single family, and all had died as toddlers in the early 1900s. I knelt down next to him and we scraped the lichen off the headstones with our fingernails so we could read the faded inscriptions better.

"Are you thinking we should just transplant some of these flowers?" asked Glenn.

"No, no, that's not what I mean," I said, alarmed that my reputation for frugality would make him think I'd dig flowers from a child's grave. "I think these grow from bulbs. We can buy some and plant them in the fall."

"Well, yes, we could do that." Glenn pondered one of the inscriptions. "But maybe it would be nice to transplant some . . . I mean, these are kids too . . . "

"Oh!" My face broke into a smile. "The kids can share! Thor will have a little present from some of the other children in the cemetery. And we can bring these kids pebbles from Thor's spot."

"Yes, that's what I mean," he said. "He'll be connected to the other kids." We plucked a couple of flowers, twirled them in our fingertips, and went home.

We visited Thor's grave again the next weekend. The ground had dried out, and the original cuts from the burial had re-emerged. They were at a sharp angle to the headstone and they extended into the next plot over, the one that was now for us, just as Glenn had said. We wedged some pebbles into the corners so we could find the lines again even after the cuts closed up, as they surely would over the next weeks. We would need to find those lines to plant the bulbs in the fall.

I imagined Thor as an unruly toddler. No sensible preschool teacher would bother trying to get little kids into straight lines. Much less insist that they stay in their places when their parents came to pick them up at the end of the day. Thor was sidling into our plot, unable to wait until school was out to greet us.

GLENN WAKES, SENSES THAT I'M AWAKE. HE ROLLS over, his face above mine, rubs his nose slowly up and down over mine. His eyes have deep circles, the right even more than the left. The creases in his face make him look much older than he is. So does the beard that he is growing as an experiment. The beard has lots of gray.

"You look anxious," he says.

"Sad," I say. "And mad."

"Mad?"

"I want someone to make it different, and no one will."

It's 5:15 a.m. on May 12. Thor's six-month birthday.

SPRING COMES late to Iowa. The days get longer and warmer in March, but not really warm. Long icicles hang from roofs of houses, roofs that are still heavy with snow. On sunny days, the icicles drip, and the drip creates puddles that freeze overnight into treacherous sheets of ice. In the mornings, birds chirp, happy to announce that the sun is coming up earlier, and then they struggle to find something to eat in the patches of mud that emerge, briefly, only to be covered by more snow a few days later. Apple trees bloom, sometimes before a late killing frost. The trees finally leaf out in early May, usually during the last week of classes or during finals week, adding insult to injury: we have just finished the so-called "spring semester."

Now we will have two or three weeks of nice weather before summer descends: hot, humid, but often too dry for the farmers, whose distressed reports of drought we begin hearing just a few weeks later.

A year ago at this time we had no idea that a five-hundred-year flood was about to ravage the eastern half of the state. A year ago at this time we had no idea I would deliver a dead child.

I CRY as I prepare breakfast. Glenn asks: "Is there anything I can do?"

I take in a breath. "I'd feel better if you weren't on the computer."

He slams it shut—gently, but still a slam.

"I'm sorry," I say, voice rising. "I'm sorry." I try not to cry. "It makes me think of you being on the computer when I was in labor. I don't want to think about that."

He swallows the accusation, comes to hold me.

AFTER BREAKFAST, after hanging up laundry.

"I'm going to check my email," I say, sullenly. "So I can't tell you that you shouldn't be on your computer."

"No, that's OK, I was going to continue reading this dissertation."

"Are you mad at me?"

"Not really." He sighs, looks up. "I wish I had nothing else to do this morning. I would spend it with you."

"I know. You can't do anything about it."

He gathers himself. "Just so . . . just to say, I wasn't just checking my email this morning, I was using the chance to send you a reminder about the lawn mower, like you asked me to."

"Yeah, I didn't mean you were doing anything bad on email."

"I know, I know," a little embarrassed that he'd brought it up. "It's fine, whatever."

I FEEL the desire to slip away to campus while he's showering, without saying goodbye. To insert some untypical behavior, as a reminder that this is *not as it should be*. Thor has been dead six months, and everyone is going to treat this as a day like any other day.

I GO upstairs. Glenn has just gotten out of the shower and dried. He comes to the steps, naked.

"I'm going now."

He sits on the step opposite me, at my height, looks into my eyes. The circles under his eyes are smoothed now. He looks refreshed. So easily.

I start to cry. "I'm sorry if I say things that make it worse for you."

He keeps looking at me. "It's OK," he says, choking back, eyes filling. "I love you. I love you." He kisses me over and over. I can't kiss back but accept his kisses.

I walk downstairs, pick up my bags, and head to the garage. I wheel out my bike and ride to work under the patchy, green trees that don't yet know whether this year will bring drought or flood.

10

THERAPY IS THE SOCIALLY SANCTIONED WAY TO deal with grief, at least among the professional classes. It's funny when you think about how recently therapy was a shameful secret. But now it's mandatory.

My friends kept wanting me to see a therapist. I saw three— four if you count Barb, who checked "grief counseling" on the insurance form.

I saw the first therapist on the day after we came home from the hospital. Glenn's regular appointment with his therapist happened to be on that day. I didn't want to go home alone after our visit to the funeral parlor. So I went with him to see Francesca.

Francesca had the neutral, concerned face that so many therapists have, and straight, light brown hair that hung to her shoulders. She led us into her dimly lit office and asked how I was doing.

Then Glenn's cell phone rang. It was his mother, who was trying to make flight reservations for the memorial service. Glenn spent the rest of the hour on the phone with her. He took a couple of breaks while she talked to the ticket agent on another line, and during the breaks the three of us—Glenn, Francesca, and I—tapped our fingers waiting for her to call back. When she did, Glenn buried himself in his phone, leaning over it confidentially, turning his head away from Francesca and me, though we could hear every word. It reassured him to take care of his mother. Yesterday his baby had died.

Francesca stared at her hands. I stared at my belly. I was trying to get used to its new size. The fact that there was no baby in there. The way the fabric of my pants rubbed against my floppy skin.

"Nice," I told him afterward, as we walked out of the office into a day so bright it seemed to mock anyone who had reason to be unhappy. "What's the point of going to therapy if whatever random call you get during that hour automatically takes priority?"

"She needed to make her reservations."

"That couldn't wait an hour, till we were done?" I stormed across the parking lot. Glenn scrambled to keep up.

"She had the agent on the other line, and he said she had to book it on that call or she'd lose the seats."

"Oh Christ, they always have some pressure tactic." I turned sharply to the right, onto the sidewalk alongside the dark brick building, and kept walking. I had no idea where I was going. "What if she hadn't happened to have called the airline till an hour later in the first place?"

"Listen, she was anxious and thought she had to do it now, and it was less stressful for me just to take care of it than to try to talk her into waiting."

"Well, I really enjoyed sitting there for an hour with Francesca, both of us wondering what we were supposed to do. She looked about as uncomfortable as I felt. Oh, right, except she didn't have a stillbirth yesterday and she wasn't coming from a meeting with the director of the fucking funeral home that's going to bury her baby . . ."

"Listen, I'm sorry, I realize this wasn't exactly ideal timing . . ."

". . . but it was less stress just to help your mother out than to ask her if you could call back, and the people who happen to be in the room with you don't count as 'stress,' I guess."

Glenn looked sideways at me. He hadn't shaved in three days. He looked worn down.

I stopped walking. "Sorry," I said.

He stepped in front of me and put his hands on my shoulders. "I'm sorry too. I don't know what to do in this situation either. It's not like I have a lot of experience with this."

God, I hate being physically restrained. I jerked out from under his hands.

"What do you want to do now?" I asked. "Should we get lunch?"

The day before, a few minutes after they'd taken Thor away, the nurse had asked if she could do anything for me. I'd told her I was hungry. "Wow, that's the last thing I expected to hear," she'd said. Apparently you're supposed to lose your appetite if your baby dies. I'd ordered Raisin Bran and a banana.

"Yeah, let's get lunch," Glenn said. "Home, or do you want to go somewhere?"

I didn't want to go back home yet, to our gloomy four walls. I didn't want to go downtown, where we might run into someone we knew. We went to the falafel place across the street, giving the empty stroller waiting outside the door a kick. The co-owner of the restaurant had a baby, though he was no better a person than we were.

THE SECOND therapist was unintentional. Iowa City Hospice advertised a support group for survivors of miscarriage, stillbirth, and infant death. It was going to meet in early December. I suspected a support group wouldn't be my thing but thought I'd go, see what it was like, in case it turned out to be good.

I was the only person to show up. The facilitator, Claudia, told me she'd been on the job about six months, and this was how it always was. Sometimes no one showed up, sometimes one person. The record had been two—that had happened once. She didn't think they were going to keep the group going much longer.

It turned out that Claudia and I had a mutual friend in DC. Shira had told Claudia to look me up when she'd moved to Iowa City that summer, but she hadn't gotten around to it.

"We could just have a one-on-one session, if you want," she said. "We offer individual counseling as well."

"Sure," I said. "I'm here anyway." I liked the idea of talking to someone who was indirectly in my circle. The fact that I'd had no personal connection to previous therapists had always seemed weird to me. I wanted to share my life with people whose lives I wanted to share and who wanted to share their lives with me.

What I mean to say is, I wanted friends.

Claudia handed me a plate of banana bread. "So," she said sadly, "I am just so sorry." Her eyebrows sloped sharply, as if to say, "I feel your pain."

"Yeah," I said. "Thanks." I chewed my banana bread and looked at her. "I'm not really sure what to say. I hadn't geared up for an individual session."

"Well, why don't you tell me how you're coping. Are you getting support, what are you doing for yourself . . ."

"Oh, sure, people are being really great—I've got the world's most supportive coworkers, I've got enough donated food in my freezer to last a year, both of our families were out for the memorial service and for Thanksgiving . . ."

"Good, good. How about you and Glenn? Are you two communicating OK?"

"Yeah, Glenn's not exactly a hold-your-feelings-in kind of guy. We've kind of developed a rhythm where we alternate bad days, or bad sections of days, so we take turns melting down and helping each other out, then switching. Though today we both had a bad day. I guess it's not a perfect system. But really, we're fine together."

"That's really great, so important" she nodded. "How about your appetite? Are you eating OK?"

I reached for another piece of banana bread. "I'm eating fine."

"Are you sleeping OK?"

"I conk out as soon as I get into bed. I may wake up for a while at three or four in the morning, but that's nothing new—that's how I always sleep."

"Are you getting exercise?"

"I started to go to the gym again." I clenched a little. "Actually, the physical thing is almost creepy. I'm so fit. The day after the stillbirth I was running errands around town; two weeks later I was running." My eyes teared up. "Really, I wish I could just have donated some of my strength to Thor—I'm so strong and he was so vulnerable."

Big sigh from Claudia. "It just doesn't seem fair, does it?"

Her eyebrows angled even more. "But you're doing OK physically, it sounds like."

She pursed her lips as if she were wondering when I was going to give her something to work with.

"Do you have times when you feel good? I mean, are there things that give you pleasure?"

"Oh, yeah, of course! Every single second I'm with Adam makes me really happy. And I'm writing a lot—I get a lot out of that. I mean, I'm usually crying as I write, but it feels really good. Does it count if you're crying? And, you know, just walking around outside, or cuddling up with Glenn, just daily stuff."

"Mmm hmm," she nodded. "But you feel like you're able to express your grief as well?"

"Well, I have at least one meltdown per day, that's a given. I cry a lot."

"So you don't feel like somehow you should be putting it behind you, or like it shouldn't still be so hard?"

I bit my tongue. Duh, no. "It hasn't even been a month! Of course it's hard. I assume it's going to be hard for months. Years."

"Good, good." Claudia approved. "A lot of what we do in grief counseling is just reassure people that it's normal to keep feeling grief, make sure they're not expecting too much of themselves."

I wondered if I was going to have to stay the whole hour.

"Are you under pressure at work? Any stress related to that?"

"No, I have a really flexible work situation. I'm not teaching this semester anyway, so I didn't have to go back to class. Other people are covering my administrative duties. I wasn't supposed to teach next semester either, but I'm going to pick up a class, so I have something to do."

Claudia studied the banana bread. She looked up at me. "You know," she said, "not everyone needs therapy."

"Yeah, I know. But it's nice to chat with you." I wished she'd just called me when she'd moved into town so we could have hung out rather than trying to be a therapist and client.

"Have you done therapy before?"

"I saw someone after my ex and I split up. That was fine, nothing exciting, mainly she asked if I was eating right and exercising and seeing friends, but it gave me some structure—to check in every couple of weeks. And I saw a therapist for a little while in Toledo, when I was in a truly awful job situation. She was pretty cool. She basically said: 'Depressed secular Jew? Have you tried Buddhism?'"

Claudia laughed. "You're doing all the right things. Exercising, eating, seeing friends, getting outside. It sounds like you don't have a lot of pressure from work, and things with Glenn are good. And the writing is really helping?"

"The writing is great."

"You know, we have a 'Writing Through Grief' group here."

"I saw that in your newsletter."

"It starts in February, I think. But you're also welcome to call any time, if you want to talk. I don't want to suggest you shouldn't. It's up to you."

"Sure, that's fine. I'll see."

Claudia smiled ruefully. "Too bad I didn't call you last summer—this isn't a great way to meet. I'm really sorry for your loss. And do come back any time."

I did. For the writing group.

THE THIRD therapist was in the summer. I was still having a hard time. Of course. But I was also busy. I'd have been writing about Thor every day anyway, but it was great to be in Iowa City, with all its outlets for writing. I'd taken the "Writing Through Grief" class at Iowa City Hospice. I'd gotten a writing coach through a program that connects graduate students at the Writers' Workshop with people who have medical stories they want to write about. I'd taken workshops at the Iowa Summer Writing Festival. All this writing about Thor! It was exactly what I wanted to be doing.

But here was the problem: I wasn't seeing a therapist, even though I wasn't all better. At least, my friends thought that was a problem. In a space of a few days, two of my best friends gave me their tough-love speeches, which basically consisted of asking how I was doing, and then when I told them things weren't easy, telling me that I needed to see a therapist and stop being so hard on my friends. They were only saying this because they loved me. But my friends couldn't do everything.

The hardest thing at this stage, I'd mentioned both times before getting this response, was the social aspect—figuring out when and with whom it was still OK to talk about Thor. People had their own lives, day-to-day stuff but also some real tragedies of their own, so Thor wasn't necessarily on their radar screen anymore, and that sometimes threw me off. But then, sometimes I discovered people thought I was shutting them out if I *didn't* talk with them about Thor.

"I'm doing a lot of writing," I'd say. "That really does a lot for me."

"Sure, but you should see a therapist."

Sometimes I tried citing medical authority to back me up.

"Iowa City Hospice has three kinds of programs: individual counseling, support groups, and writing. The writing is most helpful to me."

"Maybe you should try the support group."

"And I'm working with a writing coach through Patient Voice—that's a collaboration between the Writers' Workshop and the hospital."

"Please. Get a therapist."

I started to feel sorry for all those students getting their degrees in art therapy and music therapy. No one's going to take them seriously.

ONE OF my friends had a friend who'd seen a therapist in the Women's Wellness Center at the hospital after her own stillbirth. According to its website, the Women's Wellness Center provides counseling for women suffering from postnatal depression. *How nice that such women get a whole counseling center*, I thought crankily. *If your baby is dead, I guess you don't matter so much.* I said all this to the poor receptionist who set up my appointment later that summer. She said the staff was working toward developing a special focus on women who had miscarried or had stillbirths as well; they knew that was an issue. The therapist of the friend of my friend would be happy to see me.

This one lasted two sessions.

In our first meeting, Alice ran through the usual diagnostic checklist for depression. How I was eating. How I was sleeping. Whether I was exercising. Whether there were things that gave me pleasure. What I was doing for myself. How Glenn and I were getting along. How my thinking about the stillbirth had developed over the last months.

She nodded as I answered.

She looked as if she were waiting for me to give her something to work with.

"You know, not everyone needs therapy," she said, pushing her blond hair behind her ears. "It sounds like the writing is doing a lot for you. Is that something you do regularly?"

"I have been, really intensively. I'm shifting that a little right now. There are some work projects I want to make progress on, mainly because I want them off my desk so I can get back to the Thor stuff without anything hanging over my head."

"So you'll be doing academic writing . . . how do you think that will go?"

"I did a little in the spring. It was fine. I was glad it wasn't a huge project, but I could do it."

"So you're able to work." She flung one leg over the other.

"Yes."

"You feel good about writing about the stillbirth."

"Yes."

"Things are good with Glenn and Adam, and you're doing well physically."

"Yes."

She folded her hands.

"Why are you here?"

"I'm having trouble with my friends."

She leaned forward, interested. "What kind of trouble?"

"It's hard to know how to talk to them about this. Sometimes it really does bother me if no one asks how I'm doing—

this sense that nothing ever happened, hey, it's been eight months." Alice nodded and pushed back her hair again. "But then, if they ask me how I'm doing and I'm having a bad day and I tell them so, I'm not really sure they want to hear it. They think they do, they really do mean well, but then they wonder why they're hearing this instead of a therapist. I've gotten into my worst trouble when I actually talk about how I'm doing. With friends who say they want to know."

"You said before that you feel you've had a lot of support from friends."

"Oh, definitely. They really have been great. But there's a problem transitioning from the immediate-aftermath stage to whatever we're in now."

"Let's make that our project. Two weeks? Maybe we can think of some strategies for making things with your friends work out better."

I looked forward to that.

At our next appointment Alice confirmed that I was still eating right and still sleeping well and still exercising and that Glenn and I were still getting along.

"How are things with your friends?" Alice asked.

Not much to report on that front. It was late summer, and most people were out of town.

Never mind, I thought. We could still talk about strategies for making things work better with my friends. A few helpful hints would surely come out of the sessions.

But here was the problem. I wanted to process Thor's death, not my relationships with my friends. Processing my relationships with my friends wasn't even second priority: second priority was Glenn and Adam. I just wanted my friends to be there, or not be there, but I certainly didn't want to do relationship work with them, or see a therapist to help me do relationship work with them. This appointment—driving here, parking, filling out forms, waiting till Alice was ready for me, finding my car when we were done, driving back—had taken a big chunk out of my day. This was time I could have been writing about Thor. Or doing some other work, so I would feel easier if I wanted to spend the next day writing about Thor. Or going for a run on the route that took me by Thor's grave, where I might have stopped to chat with him. This was now the second time I'd frittered away half a day like this. The third, if you count the time I arrived at the hospital and they told me my appointment had mysteriously been cancelled, no, they couldn't explain what had happened, but perhaps I'd like to reschedule for later in the week?

I didn't go back.

But I did stop talking to my friends about Thor.

THERE ARE many honest answers to the question, "How are you doing?"

"Better—my cold's gone."

Or: *"Busy. I'm teaching a new course this semester."*

Or: *"I'd be a lot happier if it would finally stop raining and I could get back on my bike."*

They're all part of the truth, and no one will tell you you're being too hard on your friends if you say you're glad your cold is gone, or feel that you're asking more than they can give if you tell them you're teaching a new course. And so, you become publicly normal again.

I now understood: Thor really did exist for our family alone.

Glenn had insisted on an open casket and I had written Thor's biography for the funeral program, but after that summer, we lived in a public world in which I had one child, who was now working for a contractor, now traveling to Berlin, now starting college. The second child had vanished.

It was a mutually reinforcing process. I stopped mentioning Thor, stopped talking about my grief and Glenn's, because the only guarantee that a conversation would not go wrong was to have no conversation at all, and I couldn't risk having a conversation go wrong. My friends probably thought they were taking their cues from me: I wasn't talking about Thor, so they shouldn't either.

But they were surely relieved as well. It's easier to affirm your friendship by asking about the kid who's off to college than by asking about the kid who's dead.

IN AUGUST, I GOT PREGNANT AGAIN. I WASN'T IN THE least bit surprised. I was a fertility goddess, wasn't I? Still, Glenn and I high-fived each other when the nurse confirmed it.

We'd had to delay trying for another pregnancy for a few months because I'd needed to have minor surgery on my cervix, unrelated to the stillbirth. I hadn't recognized the doctor, but she'd recognized me: she'd been the attending obstetrician the night Thor was born. As she'd talked the resident through the procedure on my cervix—"OK, swab off the blood so you can get a good view"—she'd tried to pay me a compliment by describing me to the resident. "Lisa's a tough cookie. She had her cervix stitched with no anesthetic after a birth. A tough cookie." I'd wished she'd stop calling me a cookie. I'd wished she'd talk directly to me about that night. I'd wished she hadn't been there and I didn't have to wonder, while undergoing an intimate procedure I didn't want to have, what she thought, really, of the woman who had chosen a home birth and then shown up with a dead baby in the hospital.

But now that was over. I was pregnant.

I laughed, once we were back home, because I realized I hadn't fully taken it in. I'd suspected I was pregnant, because usually my breasts got tender before my period and that wasn't happening, even though my period was due. I'd taken to practically pummeling my breasts to see if I could detect any tenderness, and eventually had to wonder whether the slight pain I was feeling was due to my self-inflicted bruises. But no—truly no tenderness.

That night, after the nurse confirmed I was pregnant, Glenn, light on his feet and joyous, wrapped his arms around my hips and picked me up and spun me about. "Careful," I'd joked, feeling my belly press to his chest, "you don't want to smush anything in there!" That was when I laughed, because I realized I'd been locating my pregnancy in my breasts till then, and only now did I remember that really, the pregnancy was a bit lower than that.

It was great timing, I joked. The perfect academic year pregnancy: it was August now, and the baby would come at the end of April. Better yet, I winked to Glenn: this meant the baby would turn two *before* I turned fifty, with only one ovulation cycle to spare. That seemed wise.

I DIDN'T consider this a lucky break—I'd expected it, counted on it. Already the previous winter, not three months after Thor had died, I'd talked to the new baby, the baby I'd assumed would come.

Now it was late summer, and Würmchen—Little Worm—really was there. But I wasn't surprised to be pregnant. I'd known all along that Würmchen would come. Thor had left his room behind for her, and a little bit of fairy dust. It was just a matter of waiting till she was ready.

STORIES LIKE this are supposed to end with the woman having a baby, aren't they? Or maybe the baby doesn't actually come in this story, because that next baby isn't the subject of this story, but you know that the woman went on to have another baby and everything went fine the second time around. The woman and her partner will always be sad about their lost child; that lost child will always be with them, but their day-to-day life now is the one they'd wanted: the busy and joyous life of a couple in love and parenting a child.

A living baby, in the end, commands more attention than a dead one.

In the reproductive endocrinology clinic, the jovial doctor with the brightly colored cap said, "We had another woman in this clinic who wrote about her stillbirth, like you're doing. She got pregnant again, had the baby. They're doing great now."

Isn't that how it's supposed to happen?

12

THERE'S AN OLD PEAR TREE IN OUR BACKYARD. IT'S too close to the house. One of these days, a windstorm will blow one of the high branches onto the roof, and I'll wish we'd had it removed earlier. Already, windstorms have taken down the three ancient apple trees that were on the property when Julia and I bought it, years before Glenn moved in. The pear tree is very sick. The center is nearly hollow, and you can see the rot in the branches. It's only a matter of time.

But I hate the thought of chopping it down. It's the last of the old trees in the yard. It blossoms early in the spring, and if there's a late snow overnight, then the next morning you can look out the window to see branches full of delicate white flowers dusted with snow. When the tree leafs out it provides the only shade we have in the back yard. Then the pears ripen. No matter how ripe they get, they are as hard as bricks. You can't penetrate them with your teeth. So we don't pick them. Instead, they fall to the ground, where they attract yellow jackets. It used to be Adam's job to pick up the fallen pears and dump them in the compost. He was scared of the yellow jackets until he figured out that if he waited till after dusk, the yellow jackets would be gone.

An old man used to come by to pick the pears. He had known Bucky Bock, who had lived in the house till he died in

1993. Bucky's grandfather had built the house for his daughter's wedding in the late nineteenth century, and Bucky and his brother Lester lived there till they died—neither of them ever married. Bucky outlived Lester, and he died in the house he had been born in, by which I mean that he had a Franklin stove in the kitchen, and a cistern and outhouse in the backyard. Somewhere along the line, the city had required that he build an indoor toilet, so he did, in the basement, and the first time it plugged up was the last time he used it. As he got older and more infirm, the outhouse migrated closer and closer to the house.

After Bucky died, the house—a shack, really—went up for auction, and an architect bought it. He modernized it and built on a couple of additions, and then his wife got Parkinson's and they had to move into a condo that required less care. So Julia and I bought it.

My first couple of years there, when I was out in the yard, old men would drive by in old pickup trucks, stop, wave me over to them, squint at me, and say, "So, *you* moved into this house."

"Yes, I did," I'd say.

They'd squint harder, and ask: "Did you know Bucky Bock?"

"Nope, I never met him."

Then the old men would tell me their stories about Bucky Bock. Most of them involved the indignity of his last years, when he was refused admission to the senior center because he didn't wash. The old men hated that. Bucky had cut their hair at his barbershop when they were little kids. He and his brother had taken care of themselves all those years, hardworking guys, never hurt a fly, though Bucky was probably what they used to call feeble-minded. And then these young girls at the senior center, who didn't know a thing about life, had the nerve to throw him out.

I'd nod and mull over the story.

The next question was usually: "You got any use for them pears?"

I didn't. One old man asked if he could take them, and I said yes. He fed them to his hogs—he said it made their meat sweet. After a couple of years he stopped coming. I figured he must have died. But then another man showed up, with grimy pants and crooked, plastic-rimmed glasses. He asked: "Did you know Bucky Bock?" I said no, I hadn't known him. Then he asked: "You got any use for them pears?"

For several years he came to gather the pears. He disapproved of me, because I didn't want them. I should make pear juice out of them, he said. Pear juice had wonderful qualities. It would keep you from getting cancer, cure your gout, prevent arthritis, scare away senility. I was a fool not to make pear juice from all those pears. He was a pretty cranky old man, but if he wanted the pears, he was welcome to them.

WHEN THEY discovered on the ultrasound that Würmchen was dead, they didn't say so; they pretended they needed to do more tests. The ultrasound technician said, "I'm just going to take a look at your ovaries to give your uterus a chance to relax." Ha ha. I'd seen that shot of my uterus, with the longish blob less well-defined around the edges than it had been at my previous ultrasound three weeks earlier, and with no heartbeat. I didn't say anything. I let them stall.

When they returned to my uterus, they were very, very sympathetic. They told me how sorry they were. They didn't use the word "dead": they said, "We can't find a heartbeat." The technician patted my knee and gave it a little squeeze. They told me again how sorry they were. The physician's assistant touched my arm. She told me the size indicated a gestational age of seven weeks, six days, though I was ten weeks pregnant: Würmchen had been dead for a while.

The physician's assistant went over my options with me. I chose misoprostol. We discussed timing; I would take it the next day.

They handed me a folder from Touching Hearts, the hospital's resource for survivors of miscarriage, stillbirth, and infant death. They seemed a little embarrassed and told me I didn't need to read the stuff in it right away. I told them it was no problem, I knew Touching Hearts.

I WENT for a run after returning from the hospital and walked into the house to find Glenn taking off his jacket. "Did you just go running?" he asked. "I was about to go too."

He didn't know yet. I put my arms around his neck and tilted my head back to look up at him. "Würmchen is dead."

He closed his eyes, turned his head away and down, like he was avoiding a blow coming at him in slow motion. He turned his head back leaned his forehead against mine and started to cry. "Fuck," he said, "fuck. It's not fair."

"I know," I said.

AFTER DINNER, Glenn and I went for a walk. It was a clear night with an almost-full moon, but no one was outside, as if the slight drop in temperature that we took to signal fall signaled to everyone else that it was time to hibernate for the winter. We walked to Happy Hollow Park, where Glenn saw himself chasing ghosts of children across the grass, pushing ghosts of children on the swing, waiting to catch ghosts of children coming down the slide. We walked to City Park, and I told Würmchen we were right by the river, which was high for that time of year, and flowing fast, but not so fast as after the flood that had been there when I'd taken walks with Thor inside me.

As we headed back, Glenn asked, "Do you want to bury Würmchen in the yard?" We wouldn't really be burying Würmchen, of course. We'd be burying some sort of symbolic Würmchen. But we wanted to do that.

"I thought we could bury her with Thor," I said.

"OK," said Glenn. He was silent for a moment. "What should we bury her in? Should we get a little box?"

"We could do that," I said. "Or maybe just a shroud. A little piece of cloth, a handkerchief or something."

"Sure," Glenn said. "That would be fine."

I thought a moment. "No, I don't like that. It seems kind of . . . rough. Dry. We need something soft, like what Würmchen's used to."

"Like what?"

We walked a few more steps, away from the river and by a softball field. "A pear, from the tree. We can hollow it out, put in some sage from the garden, like we did for Thor."

"If that works for you . . ." Glenn had to process this for a moment. Then he cocked his head. "You know, I like it. There's something kind of mythical about it."

"Like a little elf, or a fairy," I said. "Maybe we should let it float down the river. Isn't that what elves do? No more burying babies underground, where there's no air or sunlight." I choked and looked back at the river.

"I don't think the pear will work. It would sink. But we could make a little boat."

That was unrealistic. "No, let's stay with the pear. It's from our yard." Besides, if we sent Würmchen down the river, she and Thor wouldn't be together, and I'd already promised both of them that they would be.

WÜRMCHEN WENT quickly. Mild cramps, the feeling of soft warmth exiting my body. And then it was over.

THE OLD man didn't come last year or this to collect the pears. Three summers ago, the last summer he came to collect pears, he looked pretty tottery. He was still wearing the same grimy pants and the same crooked glasses he'd worn the first time I met him. We got very anxious when we came home one day to see our ladder leaning against the tree—he had taken it from the garage to reach some of the pears that were higher up. I pinned a note to the tree saying he was welcome to the pears, but I'd rather he not use the ladder because I worried about him falling.

This autumn we will have the pear tree taken down. No one needs the pears any more; they just attract yellow jackets. And one day, if we leave it, a branch will come down onto the roof of the house, and we'll wish we'd had it removed earlier.

13

THE DAY BEFORE THOR'S FIRST BIRTHDAY, I READ ON Facebook: Lulu took her first steps.

The day before Thor's first birthday, I read on Facebook: Meghan had her first birthday. Her father reminisced: one year ago today, he played music while Katie groaned in the hot tub, and twelve hours later the midwife told him Meghan was coming out and he should catch her. "Happy Birthday, Meghan," he said on Facebook.

After Joe caught Meghan, I called Deirdre to tell her I was in labor. She came over and examined me. I had a while to go. She had just attended a long delivery and went home to get some rest. While she was gone my placenta tore from my uterus and Thor died. Happy birthday, Thor.

Glenn and I sit at the breakfast table. It is silent, except for the sound of ripping envelopes as Glenn works through the stack of bills. He sneezes once in a while. Adam once called Glenn's sneezes "frightening." They rip a shrieking hole through the quiet and then dissipate, leaving the room stiller than before. A cat treads stealthily across the room, curls up in a spot of sunlight, naps.

I IMAGINE Thor in his high chair at the table, between Glenn and me. He is unaware that today is different from any other day. One-year-olds don't know anything about birthdays. Glenn and I are telling Thor the story of his birth, interrupting each other, laughing. Thor is gurgling and aiming his rubber-coated spoon at his mouth, but it lands more often on his cheek. He catches Glenn's eye, and Glenn puffs up his cheeks and makes his eyes buggy. Thor laughs and waves his arms around, and applesauce dribbles from his spoon down his arm. He reaches his spoon into his bowl, and the heel of his hand clonks onto the tray. The tray vibrates, and a little square of bread skitters off the edge of the tray and onto the floor.

Thor is bereft! He leans over the side of the tray after the bread, but he cannot reach it. Thor gasps little hiccupping gasps, twists and reaches but cannot get the bread. Then he panics: he may never get his bread back! Thor screams and beats his tray with his fists, one of which lands on the edge of his bowl, which flips over and bounces upside down on the tray before falling to the floor, spraying applesauce onto my sweater on its way. I pull up the sweater to lick off the spots of applesauce, watery and sweet. Glenn picks Thor up—"Thor, did you lose your bread?" he asks rhetorically but sympathetically—and Thor screams louder: now the rest of his bread is far away too, back on his tray, and the way Daddy is holding him, he has to twist around even to see it.

Seth, the fat orange tabby, looks briefly at the chaos above, saunters to the bread on the floor, and nibbles at it. I walk to the kitchen to fetch a sponge to clean up the applesauce and trip over gray and white Fo Fum, who is looking dumbly at his paw. The tortoise shell, Fee Fi, wants some bread, too, and sees that the situation is as it always is: orange fatty gets all the

goodies. Fee hisses at Seth, Seth looks up good-naturedly—
he never understands what the problem is—and Fee smacks
him across the face. Thor cries louder, though not because of
the evolving catfight—Thor is oblivious to the action below—
and Glenn bounces him. I crawl between Glenn's legs to get at
the source of the catfight, to remove the bread. I set my hand
into a puddle of applesauce and skid in Fee's direction; Fee
turns tail and runs, pausing on the way to the kitchen to hiss
once more at Seth, who is crawling, undeterred, under my arm
to get the bread I have not yet picked up. Tabby Mabel looks
in briefly from the kitchen, confirms that she's too mature for
all this nonsense, and proceeds to the windowsill in the dining
room.

The news blares in the background. I ask Glenn if he can
turn it off—the noise is rattling my brain. He can't hear me
over Thor's screaming and asks me, loudly, what I said. I holler
back, "Can you turn off the radio?" Glenn cranes his head to
avoid Thor's flailing arms, but one of them hits, and Glenn's
glasses careen to the floor, flipping a couple of times on the
way. I pick them up, stand, hand them to Glenn, reach for
Thor.

"C'mon, Thor, let's go outside." I slide the glass door and
step onto the back porch, and cool air hits my face. Thor is
still crying, but there are no cats hissing, no radio blaring, no
Glenn sneezing, no parents shouting at each other to be heard.
It is chilly outside and there are things to distract Thor: the
locust tree, the bird feeder, the leaves whose crunching under-
foot begs for a toddler to stomp on them.

IT'S THOR'S first birthday, and we eat breakfast in silence. Glenn taps at his laptop. Despina has sent a message of condolence, and Glenn wants to answer it right away. Tap tap tap. Lulu's parents have also sent a message. The refrigerator hums. I pour milk into my coffee. Seth gallops up to the sliding doors to be let in. In the garden bed, outside the window, the yellow asparagus fronds wave in the November breeze.

THAT AFTERNOON, we visit Thor's grave. We want to exchange the summer decorations for the winter decorations. But as we approach, we see: there will be a graveside service that afternoon, right on Thor's row, just a few spots away. A canvas canopy stretches over folding chairs; at the front is a plain pine box on a stand that can be moved after the service to the grave, so the coffin can be lowered. Glenn and I puzzle over this: will they bring the dead body wrapped in a sheet and put it in the box here, outside, in front of all the guests? No, we decide: the body will arrive in its coffin, and they will put the coffin into the box. Or maybe the box is just a placeholder, and when the coffin arrives, they will take off the box and replace it with the coffin. That's probably it: the plain wooden box can't possibly be the coffin for this burial. The headstone had gone up just a couple of days earlier, and it is an enormous, showy thing: polished black granite, tapering at the top to a rounded point, almost as tall as I am. Someone with that kind of headstone doesn't get buried in a plain wooden box.

We have become connoisseurs of the *things* of death.

A man from the cemetery staff is standing about, making sure everything remains in order until the guests arrive. He pulls his jacket tighter around his neck and tells us we might want to move our car so it doesn't get blocked in when everyone arrives for the burial. That's OK, we say. We don't have a car here, we walked.

We decorate Thor's grave. The chimes come down, jangling loudly in protest until I grab the metal tubes with my hand and they clunk a choked final chord. The birdfeeder goes up, and we fill it with sunflower seeds. We lash a sheaf of tall grasses to the shepherd's crook. The grasses came from Shell and Ann's farm in Wisconsin. We'd done the same thing last year, when we'd visited the farm not quite a month after Thor's death: our first trip after the birth, the infant seat still in a large plastic bag in the garage. Ever since, we'd brought Thor souvenirs from our travels, anxious efforts to placate our guilt for traveling without him, for going on without him. Seashells from California. Pinecones from Minnesota.

We sit on the ground next to Thor and read to him. Julia stops by: she had been jogging through the woods behind the cemetery and had wondered if we would be here. She sits with us as we read some more, and then goes.

The funeral guests begin to arrive. They are burying a firefighter. His nickname had been "Man of Steel," and his death had been front-page news. There are fire trucks, bagpipes, uniformed men and women who stand in military formation and salute as the coffin is lowered from the fire truck to the stand. It is senseless to try to continue our quiet reading to Thor. And so we tell Thor about all the activity, as if it were a big birthday party just for him. I describe the people and the music and the uniforms and the headstone—"To tell you the truth, it looks a little phallic to me," I whisper behind my hand to Thor, as the bagpipes blare. Sure, breakfast was pretty frustrating, with all those bread squares falling on the floor and the cats snarfing them up. But now there are fire trucks! What a birthday!

As we stand up to go, Glenn casts a long look at Thor's grave, at the marigolds still blooming on either side of Thor's headstone, deep red, orange, and yellow. They won't last much longer: it's already mid-November. "Maybe," he puts his hands on his hips, leaning his head toward his right shoulder in resignation, "maybe some people from the burial will have noticed us here, and will be curious and come by afterward, and see that it's Thor's birthday." The Man of Steel and his fire trucks and bagpipes and salutes have cut short our time with Thor. But there's nothing to be done about it. "Maybe they'll stop by and notice that a baby died, and think about Thor too," Glenn says. It's the best he can muster.

VI

Children, Transported

TWELVE DAYS AFTER THOR WAS SUPPOSED TO BE born, he was born.

Twelve days after Thor was born and died, we buried him.

Twelve days after James was born—right on schedule—he came to live with us.

IN THE spring after the stillbirth, around the time I was having surgery on my cervix, we started investigating adoption again. We let the state know we were open to adoptions from the foster care system. And we found a miraculous little agency in northern Iowa, which operated out of an old public school and had a web page barely worthy of the name because they weren't trolling for clients; they weren't looking to make money. They were looking to help pregnant women. Avalon suited us: they helped pregnant women get whatever kind of help they wanted, whether it was an abortion, assistance in raising a child, or placement of the child in an adoptive family. We suited Avalon: they didn't mind that we were over forty, unmarried, and not Christian. And, a year and a half later, we suited Jasmine: we traveled a lot, we were educators, we welcomed African American children, we wanted to adopt though I had a kid about to go to college, we seemed somehow . . . unorthodox, and she liked that. Jasmine had her baby, and then hoped fervently that we would want it, which we did, and James came to us.

James was awake, and then he slept. He was hungry, then sated. He cried, then he was content, and then he cried again.

The first time we showed him the kitties he got hungry, and the second time he fell asleep.

And then, slowly, he learned that kitties, unlike tables, are animate beings, who move and meow of their own volition. Who come toward him and go away from him. Who sometimes hiss at each other in a way that frightens him, but sometimes sweetly groom each other.

Now, at six months, he understands that kitties have fur that is sometimes orange, sometimes black, sometimes white or gray or speckled, but always soft.

Now, at six months, he laughs with muscles tightened around his lips as if he were about to insert an oboe and let out a perfect "A," and the entire orchestra will tune to his command.

Now, at six months, he reaches with both hands for his bare feet and inserts one, then the other, into his mouth.

Now, at six months, he awaits only a court date until he is officially Glenn's and my child.

This is my life now: the life of a working mother of a six-month-old and a nineteen-year-old. Introducing solid foods. Laughing at baby giggles. Playing an undeclared game of chicken with Glenn about who will break down first and change a diaper. Prepping for class. Booking flights to visit Adam at college in LA. Correcting page proofs of a book that has been in production far too long. Calling the babysitter to see if she can stay an extra hour. Answering questions in departmental meetings. Reviewing manuscripts for some journal or other. Picking the first asparagus of the season. Watching Glenn and James Skype with Glenn's sister. Reading Adam's Facebook posts. Wrapping James in the baby carrier so he can rest against my chest as I hang up the laundry. Unclipping the carrier—quietly—to lay a sleeping baby down on the bed to finish his nap.

A live baby, after all, commands more attention than a dead one.

James is a happy story. But he is not the happy ending to the story in this book. This book is about a dead baby, and there is nothing happy about a dead baby. Not beginning, not middle, not end.

I do not need to write James's story. Someday he, like Adam, will be able to write his own book, animate his own film, choreograph his own dance, direct his own play.

Thor will not be able to do those things, and so I must do them for him. I must create memories where there are none. I must create a life where there is none.

And I am inadequate to the task. Two and a half years after his death, I have trouble pulling up memories of that time. Brain memories, yes; I can tell you what happened. But heart memories only rarely. Only at strange and unexpected moments—reading a gently twisting sentence in a book, finding the maternity pants I'd donated to Goodwill back on the same sales rack where I'd originally bought them, hearing birds chatter as I glimpse a hot air balloon against a still, clear sky—only then does my throat catch as I remember the feelings from those days.

It's supposed to be comforting to know that overwhelming grief will not last forever, that it will fade and you'll feel normal again, that sadness will become something that remains within measure rather than covering the universe.

It's certainly practical that this happens. It makes it more tolerable to correct page proofs for a book that has been in production far too long. It's even good that this happens: it makes it possible to laugh at baby giggles.

But it's no comfort. Even when I was in my deepest despair about Thor's death, I feared the day that despair would lessen, because I knew it would feel like a betrayal: a betrayal of a child already grievously betrayed. Thor has no life; the least I can do is give him my passion. And as the despair has lessened, I do that less and less. All I can do is write what I remember fast, before it all disappears.

2

I OFTEN WISHED THOR WOULD COME TO VISIT ME IN
a dream, since that was the only place I could see him. I told
him I'd be so happy if he'd do that. Once in a while, he did.

One night, three and a half months after Thor's birth and
death, I was restless. It was around four in the morning, and
the first bird to wake up was beginning to chirp: a confident
solo with spacing between tones that suggested that neither
song nor silence was to be feared. I wanted to have Thor next
to me in his bassinet, and I also wanted my editor to answer
my emails, in about equal measure at that moment. I went to
the bathroom, and when I came back to bed, Glenn asked how
I was doing. "Not so good," I said.

"Stomachache?" Glenn asked.

"No, head. Psyche."

Glenn probably had a fleeting moment of dread. I'd had
a "psyche" moment just a few nights earlier, angsting about
Adam. Glenn told me a visualization exercise he'd learned from
his sister Ellen. Put your cares in a balloon, tie it up, and let it
float gently into the sky. Then sleep in peace, and come back
to whatever's ailing you in the morning, when you're a little
more lucid.

But that night I was thinking about Thor. As I lay half
asleep and half awake, Thor became a balloon, floating into the

sky, farther and farther away. He was floating gently, but still, a little longer and he'd be out of sight entirely. He was already way above all the buildings, just a spot of color with a thin string dangling against a gentle blue sky. The only thing left for him to encounter, the only thing between him and infinity, were the clouds, little puffs drifting lazily from west to east, as they do in Iowa. But by the time he reached them, he'd already be too far away for me to see. And what if a storm came up? Thor was all by himself, untethered, bobbing aimlessly along. There would be no one to scoop him up and rush him inside or hold him tight against the rain and wind. He'd be pelted with rain. He'd get cold. He'd break.

I looked at the balloon with the kind of longing and loss and frustration of a little kid who got a balloon at a fair, only to lose her grasp and see it float into the sky. For so many kids, that must be the first experience of watching an irrevocable loss as it happens, not like dropping a coin down the sewer drain where it's gone from one moment to the next, but watching, watching, as the balloon gets farther and farther away, and you know you can't have it back but you can still see it as it recedes, you *have to* watch it receding. I pulled the covers up over my head. I didn't want to see the window. I didn't want to see the sky, which was just starting to lighten. I knew I wouldn't see a balloon.

By now, more birds were awake, and they were playing chamber music. The sparrow's trill and robin's chirp were set nicely against the blue jay's distant whistle, though the crow's intermittent caw had the effect of a dropped cymbal. I became crankily jealous of the little boy in the old French movie, *The Red Balloon*. First of all, I couldn't tell what color Balloon Thor was; his shape was distinct, but his color wasn't. How nice for the little French boy, that his balloon was so close that he could see that it was red. Even better, his balloon followed him around; sometimes it even showed him where to go, and it waited for him all day long while he was in school. Sure, it was up in the air, but it was still magically tethered to him, to Paris, to the earth. Just far enough away to have some fun, to tease the boy a little, but the balloon would never, ever leave for real.

I drifted in and out of sleep. When I next woke, I thought of the evil balloons in Don Hertzfeldt's animation, *Billy's Balloon*, a cult favorite among art-animation fans like Adam. Cute little Billy, a stick figure, has a balloon. Magically, the balloon carries him up into the air, and Billy can see the earth below him. Wow! Billy is entranced. But then, the balloon lets him drop. The balloon picks him up again, takes him up, lets him drop again. Another kid shows up with her sweet little balloon, which soon starts bopping her on the head. More and more happy kids appear with balloons and by the end of the film it's a massacre. Balloons are pounding on kids, dropping them from the sky, dragging them around by their feet, taking them up so high they'll never see the earth again, running them in front of airplane engines. It's really very funny.

During one of my earlier waking moments, I had told Glenn that I wanted to sleep in, and so when he woke he slipped out of bed without me. Just before I woke for the last time that night, I dreamed of a hot-air balloon coming toward me as I lay dying, with a little boy, seven years old or so, waving and smiling. It was Thor, welcoming me. I was going to get into the balloon with him and float away to the other side. His face was open and confident: he was an old hand at the other side, and proud that he—just a little boy!—would soon be able to show me that there was nothing to fear.

I wish I could say that as I saw Thor, my eyes lightly closed to preserve his image as I woke, it was to the sound of a symphony of birds celebrating the full arrival of day: noisy, triumphant, unrestrained. But that moment had passed. By the time I recognized my dream for what it was, all the birds had to offer was a random residue of chirps carelessly strewn about like the last, insignificant breadcrumbs shaken out of a plastic bag. The bedroom window showed a dull gray sky, crushing in its ordinariness.

But I often call back that image of Thor at age seven, smiling and waving from his balloon. Not when I happen to see a hot air balloon floating by. Just when I want to see him.

And then a thousand cool sparks burst from Thor, not destructively but generatively; they race toward me, pass easily through the skin that separates me from the world; and the particles of Thor course through my veins, permeate my muscles, my fat, my ligaments; and Thor is once again inside me, of me, with me. But then I look up, and there I see Thor smiling and waving, intact and lovely in the basket that hangs from the balloon, and he is what all children should be: his own distinct self.

ACKNOWLEDGMENTS

I OWE A GREAT DEBT TO MARY ALLEN, WHO TAUGHT the first writing workshop I ever took—and who then combed through every word of this manuscript to let me know where it moved her and where it fell flat. Paula Michaels, too, gave her careful feedback on the entire manuscript. My midwife, identified in these pages as Deirdre, bravely re-engaged a painful period in her own life by reading a draft and helping me to understand her experience of Thor's death. Thanks also to Jane Gerhard, Kate Gies, and BK Loren for their comments on portions of this book.

In the immediate aftermath of Thor's death, I stumbled upon Pat Dolan's Writing through Grief course at Iowa City Hospice and Arts Share's Patient Voice Program, which matched me with writing coach June Melby. I'm grateful to have met both of them in the early stages of this project. And I'm grateful for my conversations with Jen Silverman, who made me think in new ways about grief and art.

Finally, thanks to Elizabeth Koke, Jeanann Pannasch, and Amy Scholder of the Feminist Press, and to Jack Halberstam for helping to connect me with them.

Those are my debts as author of this book, at least some of them. My home, my phone, my private email, and the occasional old-fashioned letter: those are the places for me to acknowledge my personal debts for support and understanding in the aftermath of Thor's death. I hope I've managed to do so adequately.

The Feminist Press is an independent, nonprofit literary publisher that promotes freedom of expression and social justice. Founded in 1970, we began as a crucial publishing component of second wave feminism, reprinting feminist classics by writers such as Zora Neale Hurston and Charlotte Perkins Gilman, and providing much-needed texts for the developing field of women's studies with books by Barbara Ehrenreich and Grace Paley. We publish feminist literature from around the world, by best-selling authors such as Shahrnush Parsipur, Ruth Kluger, and Ama Ata Aidoo; and North American writers of diverse race and class experience, such as Paule Marshall and Rahna Reiko Rizzuto. We have become the vanguard for books on contemporary feminist issues of equality and gender identity, with authors as various as Anita Hill, Justin Vivian Bond, and Ann Jones. We seek out innovative, often surprising books that tell a different story.

See our complete list of books at **feministpress.org**, and join the Friends of FP to receive all our books at a great discount.

THE FEMINIST PRESS
AT THE CITY UNIVERSITY OF NEW YORK
FEMINISTPRESS.ORG